The Productive Body

François Guéry and Didier Deleule

The Productive Body

François Guéry and Didier Deleule

Translated, with an introduction,

by Philip Barnard and Stephen Shapiro

Winchester, UK
Washington, USA

First published by Zero Books, 2014
Zero Books is an imprint of John Hunt Publishing Ltd., Laurel House, Station Approach,
Alresford, Hants, SO24 9JH, UK
office1@jhpbooks.net
www.johnhuntpublishing.com
www.zero-books.net

For distributor details and how to order please visit the 'Ordering' section on our website.

Text copyright: François Guéry and Didier Deleule 2013
Introduction and Translation copyright: Philip Barnard and Stephen Shapiro 2014

ISBN: 978 1 78099 576 2

A CIP catalogue record for this book is available from the British Library.

Design: Lee Nash

Printed and bound by CPI Group (UK) Ltd, Croydon, CR0 4YY

We operate a distinctive and ethical publishing philosophy in all
areas of our business, from our global network of authors to
production and worldwide distribution.

CONTENTS

Editors' Introduction
to the English Edition

Philip Barnard and Stephen Shapiro

1.

François Guéry and Didier Deleule's *The Productive Body*—originally published as *Le corps productif* in 1972—is an overlooked treasure and under-used critical pathway. This succinct volume has been a key reference hiding in plain sight, a text whose initial impact and interest for Anglophone readers today may lie in its relation to major writings by Michel Foucault, one of the most influential theorists and historians for post-1960s work in the human sciences and, at this point, a canonical figure in twentieth-century thought.

With the possible exception of *The History of Sexuality: Volume I* (1976), *Discipline and Punish: The Birth of the Prison* (1975) is the text by Foucault that is most frequently read, cited, and used in the classroom. Within this work, the section "Panopticism" is usually the most excerpted and taught. Here Foucault illustrates his larger argument about a modern form of decentralized power that operates through the intersection of professional institutions and the production of expert knowledge, by describing a model prison proposed by the English utilitarian philosopher Jeremy Bentham. The description summarizes Foucault's arguments about what he calls "discipline" as a device or set of social technologies for controlling potentially unruly lower and laboring class populations through techniques of supervisorial examination. Discipline segments time, space, and social relations through an instrumental use of small details that paradoxically also result in making larger numbers of plebian and proletarian subjects more docile and useful in the modern pursuit of profit. The disciplines "made it possible to increase the size of multiplicities...whether in a workshop or a nation, an army or school" by breaking the activities and identities of people within these organizations into smaller, more regulated categories and classifications that are supervised by a new set of managers, who assume responsibility for social engineering.

In "Panopticism," Foucault is explicit about the relationship between the invention of disciplinary techniques and the rise of capitalist exploitation.

> If the economic take-off of the West began with the techniques that made possible the accumulation of capital, it might perhaps be said that the methods for administering the accumulation of men made possible a political take-off in relation to the traditional, ritual, costly, violent forms of power, which soon fell into disuse and were superseded by a subtle, calculated technology of subjection. In fact, the two processes—the accumulation of men and the accumulation of capital—cannot be separated; it would not have possible to solve the problem of the accumulation of men without the growth of an apparatus of production capable of both sustaining them and using them; conversely, the techniques that made the cumulative multiplicity of men useful accelerated the accumulation of capital. At a less general level, the technological mutations of the apparatus of production, the division of labor and the elaboration of the disciplinary techniques sustained an ensemble of very close relations (cf. Marx, *Capital*, vol. I, chapter XIII and the very interesting analysis in Guerry and Deleule). [*Discipline*, 220-221; *sic*. Both French and English editions misspell Guéry's name and give an incorrect date of publication.]

This "very interesting analysis" is Guéry and Deleule's *Le Corps Productif* (hereafter known as *The Productive Body*). In his entire corpus, Foucault rarely mentions other contemporary writers in the conventional style of scholarly referencing. On record as personally disinclined to engage in polemical academic name-calling, there are few instances of any direct reply by Foucault to others, even when the target of his arguments is easy to discern. Conversely, Foucault was equally hesitant to formally highlight the importance of others' work for his own in this manner, perhaps so as not to appear partisan in the affirmative sense either. A long-standing criticism of Foucault's historical writing is the relative absence of the conventional scholarly apparatus of citations and footnotes that often takes up many pages in specialized monographs. Thus, given the highly unusual nature of this reference, with Foucault so clearly recommending Guéry and Deleule's text in one of the most frequently-read passages in recent critical theory, why has *The Productive Body* been left unexamined until now?

Perhaps one reason involves the lack of attention given to the entire paragraph that embeds the reference to *The Productive Body*. For much of the rise in Foucault's influence for English-language readers has come alongside, and arguably due to, the post-1960s retreat from Marx and attention to class as a category of analysis. Many Anglophone students of Foucault have been dogmatically, and wrongly, taught that Foucault was simply anti-marxist, rather than dissenting from the rigidities of the French Communist Party, of which he was briefly a member in the early 1950s. Consequently, there has been a determined will to ignorance on this question by many Anglophone acolytes of Foucault, and reluctance to read what is simply and literally written on his pages. Despite what often seems to be a nearly scholastic over-parsing of every inflection in Foucault's writing, his repeated mentions of Marx and Marx's description of capitalism have been largely ignored. Indeed, there is a particular censorial tendency registered in Anglophone collections such as *The Essential Works of Michel Foucault, 1954-1984* (3 volumes, 1998-2001), which often exclude both previously-translated pieces on Marx and left-wing activism, or the many considerations of left politics that are included in the standard four-volume collection of Foucault's shorter writings and interviews, *Dits et Écrits* (1994). The consequence of this pattern of translation and editorial selection is that Foucault's Anglophone readers have not had the opportunity to recognize that, throughout the 1970s, Foucault was engaged in a supplemental analysis of historical and contemporary capitalism. Though he has rarely been read in context of Euro-marxist debates, Foucault nevertheless attempted throughout the decade to implement and expand Marx's claims, albeit not in the conventional languages of Euro-marxism. His concept of discipline was arguably a means of further analyzing class conflict and bourgeois strategies for smashing working-class solidarity, and his exploration of governmentality can be understood as an inquiry into the mechanisms of decentralized competition among the bourgeoisie.

The Productive Body has suffered, then, from a particular Foucault-effect that seeks to erase the centrality and larger significance of Marx for Foucault's analyses. Yet Guéry and Deleule's essays have more to offer than insights into this aspect of Foucault, for they belong to the hugely generative moment of French left and "maoist" engagements in the aftermath of the student revolts of May 1968. Guéry and Deleule fashion their text locally in relation to instances of French industrial disputes during the period, and they depart from several longstanding strains of French marxism held to be insufficient, if not surreptitiously complicit with efforts to contain worker and student activism outside the institutional networks of the French Communist Party. These strands are primarily the "structuralist" marxism associated with Louis Althusser and his students such as Étienne Balibar, Pierre Macherey, and Nicos Poulantzas; and the phenomenological marxism associated with Maurice Merleau-Ponty. With its critique of psychology and the larger construction of the concept of the "individual" subject, *The*

Productive Body can also be read alongside the period's antipsychiatry writings by R.D. Laing, Thomas Szasz, and David Cooper. Yet in ways perhaps more clear to us in retrospect, Guéry and Deleule also diverge from what would later become influential strands emerging from Gilles Deleuze and Félix Guattari; the neoanarchist or autonomist writings of Antonio Negri; and a Lacanian-inflected marxism best known today through Slavoj Žižek. From today's vantage point, their study also distinguishes itself from the era's other maoist-associated writers who have recently become more widely read in Anglophone circles, such as Alain Badiou and Jacques Rancière. Most significantly, perhaps, especially in relation to the larger structuralist and poststructuralist context in which it emerged, *The Productive Body* offers a model of subjectivity that does not rest on semiotics or the "linguistic turn" associated with many structuralist and poststructuralist models, but rather on a renewed focus on the transformation of experience through and typified by the capitalist workplace.

While *The Productive Body* stands alone on the intellectual strength of its arguments, it also merits renewed interest in the current juncture, forty years after its initial appearance. Recent discussions of the rise of virtualizing and visualizing informatics, like algorithmic imaging and actuarial "Big Data," make *The Productive Body*'s caution against software prescient and as vital to read as if were a contemporary text. Moreover, today we can more clearly see fruitful directions for marxism that Guéry and Deleule began to chart, but that still remain to be pursued. For as we will discuss below, the approach they propose in this book encourages us to articulate elements of marxism with Foucault's work on knowledge, power, and institutions. Such a line of analysis avoids reliance on notions of depth subjectivity, but also escapes a somewhat giddy celebration of affects, assemblages, or fascination with the "moment" or the "encounter." *The Productive Body*, arguably like much of Foucault, grounds itself in

5

Marx's arguments about the nature of capitalism's development, but seeks to further excavate its implications for collective labor and possible modes of resistance. In this way, *The Productive Body* also speaks anew to today's readers, who face the convergence of economic regimes that dictate austerity and the normalization of precarity, alongside the rise of new technologies of data surveillance, software engineers as masters of social-system and labor control, and medical advances that seek to redesign the body through digitally-driven prosthetic devices, gene modification, and nanotechnology.

As is often the case with new approaches, *The Productive Body* can be daunting reading on first sight, especially for those who are not well versed in Marx's *Capital*, volume I. Many theory texts initially received as especially complex or challenging become increasingly legible, if not commonsensical, with the accumulation of time and secondary commentary. *The Productive Body* has not been so rewarded, however, and thus it may help first-time readers orient themselves to Guéry and Deleule's arguments with some social and historical context, an explanation of *Capital's* relevant aspects, and a succinct overview of *The Productive Body's* primary claims. Lastly, we will return to the question of why Foucault would have so unusually highlighted *The Productive Body*, and how reading it today helps reopen the walkway between Foucault and Marx for students of both.

2.

Given the many parallels in their personal and intellectual trajectories prior to 1972, it is not surprising, in retrospect, that Didier Deleule and François Guéry collaborated on *The Productive Body*, nor that they developed it at the moment they did. Both authors have Parisian origins and, during the mid and late 1960s Deleule was a student at the Sorbonne while Guéry was enrolled at the Ecole Normale Supérieure (ENS), the "haute école" that has produced large numbers of elite intellectuals and scientists from its founding during the Revolution to the present. Considering only the generational cohorts that concern us directly in this discussion, students and faculty at the Ecole Normale during these years include many key names associated with structuralist and poststructuralist debates in the human sciences and left or marxist critical theory and philosophy, including Louis Althusser, Étienne Balibar, Alain Badiou, Jacques Rancière, Jacques-Alain Miller, Pierre Bourdieu, and Jacques Derrida. Former normalien Michel Foucault was not present at the school directly, as a faculty member, in the late 1960s, but maintained a strong presence via his publications and rapidly increasing status as a leading figure of the generation. Guéry and Deleule also worked during this period with Georges Canguilhem, a notable figure in the history and philosophy of science, who, although still relatively under-appreciated in English-speaking circles, exerted a tremendous influence on this generation of French intellectuals.

Guéry and Deleule's early careers brought the two together once again when both had teaching positions that overlapped at the beginning of the 1970s at the Université de Franche-Compté in Besançon, eastern France. The project that became *The Productive Body* began when editor Gilles Anquetil, inaugurating a new book series with Editions Mâme, invited Deleule to submit a manuscript related to his work on the theoretical foundations of psychology, i.e., Deleule's 1969 book *La Psychologie; mythe scientifique* and his 1971 articles on the philosophy of psychology (see Bibliography and Works Cited). Asked to collaborate on the volume, given their common interest in developing a genealogy of the human sciences, Guéry contributed his analysis, partly derived from and in response to several contemporary strands of marxist and philosophical questioning, of the epochal split or gulf that emerges, in industrial capitalism, between the modes of knowledge associated with manual and intellectual labor. Both Guéry and Deleule went on to careers at, primarily, the univer-

7

sities of Lyon III-Jean Moulin (Guéry) and Paris X-Nanterre (Deleule). They are both currently emeritus professors.

The lines of questioning opened up with *The Productive Body* established often-renewed threads than have run through both Guéry's subsequent work on industry and philosophy, Marx, and modern philosophy, and Deleule's on the origins of liberal political economy and its relations with philosophy and the human sciences, (Guéry and Deleule, "Réponses aux questions sur Le corps productif"; Guéry, "Dialogue pour *Le corps productif*").

Guéry and Deleule's entry into these questions took place in the rapidly evolving and often explosive social and political atmosphere that prevailed in the aftermath of May 1968 and the general strike that united French students and workers in a context of national struggle that was one important element of the larger anti-systemic revolt of the late 1960s. Two crucial elements of this context for both authors were the brief but intense intellectual and political wave of "maoism" among French students and workers, particularly at the Ecole Normale Supérieure during the authors' years there, and the related period of post-1968 student-worker solidarity that included notable events such as the Larzac regional resistance movement beginning in 1971; the murder of Pierre Overney, a "maoist" ex-factory worker, during a demonstration in February 1972; and the storied Lip watch factory strike, which built up during the post-1968 years when Guéry and Deleule were teaching in nearby Besançon, and burst into national headlines in early 1973, shortly after the publication of *The Productive Body* (readers interested in these events may consult two recent documentaries by director Christian Rouaud: *Les Lip: L'Imagination au Pouvoir*, 2007, and *Tous au Larzac*, 2011).

The "maoist" moment of French left activism during the mid and late 1960s produced intense left-theoretical debates, gave rise to several short-lived groups and publications, and reverberated more widely in avant-garde yet relatively mainstream and visible outlets, from the key journal *Tel Quel* to widely-viewed *nouvelle vague* films such as Jean-Luc Godard's *La Chinoise* (1967). The movement's history is complex in its detail (for useful historical overviews, see Fields, "French Maoism," and Bourg, "The Red Guards of Paris") and "controversial" in the strict sense of the word, as it continues to elicit conflicting historical interpretations and even renewed partisan polemics. Contemporary polemics concerning this episode often emerge from a generation facing retirement and engaged in self-reflection, and debate the movement's relevance as a model for the ongoing anti-neoliberalism campaigns of younger activists and scholars.

As a student at the Ecole Normale Supérieure, Guéry in particular was directly exposed to and surrounded by the movement, its arguments, and several of its notable actors, because a group of students at the ENS, initially (but not ultimately) supported by Althusser in their rejection of PCF orthodoxy, converged to form a maoist-oriented *Cercle d'Ulm* (The Ulm Circle, referring to the rue d'Ulm where the ENS is located). This ENS-based group in turn exerted considerable influence within two of the moment's most important communist student groups: the UEC (*Union des Etudiants Communists*, Union of Communist Students) and the UJC(ML), or *Union des Jeunesses Communistes (Marxistes-Leninistes)*, the Union of Communist Youth, which was formed when maoist elements were purged from the UEC.

For our purposes, two aspects of the movement are relevant to *The Productive Body*. First, the maoism in question, i.e., the movement's identification with the Chinese Cultural Revolution, was in many ways less concerned with matters Chinese (despite the period's sloganeering and fascination with Mao), than with a rejection or delegitimation, on the part of communist and other left radicals, of the French Communist Party (PCF). The groups

9

that, in late 1960s France, called themselves maoist, tended toward anti-hierarchical and semi-autonomous forms of organization, rejecting what they saw as the PCF's doctrinaire ("Stalinist"), USSR-oriented institutional and theoretical positions, which were often felt to be insufficiently attentive to cultural matters. The ENS movement generated a small wave of theoretical reconsiderations of partisan marxism that coincided and indeed overlapped, in a dialectical manner, with the group that worked in Althusser's *Reading Capital* project ("The Red Guards of Paris," 481-82).

Second, a central concern of the "maoist" groups, particularly as the movement evolved after 1968 with the founding of the GP or *Gauche Prolétarienne* (Proletarian Left), was the question of the division of labor and an ensuing focus on questions of hierarchy, production, and technology, and the modes of inequality and alienation they generate ("French Maoism," 169-70). The notable moments of French social and political resistance and organization in the early 1970s mentioned earlier—the Larzac resistance movement, the strikes associated with the murder of Pierre Overney, and the Lip watch factory strike and episode of worker autonomy—all occasioned intensive reflection on these themes.

Hence the French maoist moment of the late 1960s provided a context that contributed on several levels to Guéry and Deleule's focus on (1) the problematic of the split between intellectual and manual labor, and (2) the question of the functionality and utility of this split in controlling and subordinating labor to capital. The authors additionally frame these two questions as significant problems in the intellectual-institutional genealogy of the human sciences; but certainly maoist concerns with the nature and implications of the division between manual and intellectual labor open onto the split or scission that is at the center of *The Productive Body*, figuring in both the reading of *Capital* proposed by Guéry in Part One, and the genealogy of scientific psychology proposed by Deleule in Part Two.

3.

To better appreciate Guéry and Deleule's intervention at the time of the book's publication in 1972, as well as the ways in which their positions are likewise interesting for our moment some forty years later, a basic review of their terms is helpful. *The Productive Body*'s foreword introduces the terminology and central theoretical question, or problematic, that Guéry's and Deleule's individual essays will explore. Following conventional claims by Marx, the authors begin by insisting on the intimate inter-relationship between humans and their means of production, here technology, but also energy sources and raw materials. They introduce a three-fold distinction between categories of bodies: the biological body, the social body, and the productive body. These three "bodies" are not sharply distinguished; there is an overlap and continuity between them. While each category becomes loosely associated with different periods in the development of historical capitalism, the crucial question is less the isolated definition of each category than the inter-relation of the three and the implications of the developmental pattern they outline.

The biological body is simply the human apparatus, the linkage of vitality and physiognomy that cements birth, life, work, child-creation, physical decline, and death. Although Guéry and Deleule partially imply that the biological body is the dominant form of conceptualizing the organic apparatus in the age before the onset of capitalism sometime around the late fifteenth century (a juncture signaled by the name Galileo), they do not claim that the biological body exists outside social conditions or has a fundamental essence and eternal meaning. Indeed, one of their implied complaints about marxist phenomenology is that that it falls prey to a nostalgic utopianism about authentic bodily experience uncontaminated by capitalism. While Malthus sought to establish transhistorical claims about the relationship between population and food or natural resource depletion, for

11

example, Marx insisted that "every particular historical mode of production has its own special laws of population, which are historically valid within that particular sphere. An abstract law of population exists only for plants and animals, and even then only in the absence of any historical intervention by man" (*Capital*, I:784). Likewise, Guéry and Deleule do not attempt to define any transcendental "human-ness" or authentic truths about the body and its sensory faculties. Just as Marx was less interested in questions of labor, money, and commodities in general or in the abstract, than in how labor, money, and commodities operate within *capitalist* societies, Guéry and Deleule seek to examine the shifting role of the biological body *within* capitalism. Consequently, their discussion seeks to disengage from a phenomenology that takes the human body, its sensory apparatus, and its emotions as the fundamental source of authentic experience.

Their second category, the social body, is understood as that which emerges through divisions of labor, wherein different individuals take on different tasks within a larger collective. Thus, *all* societies have modes of socialization, rituals of life passage, and labor conditions for every biological body. Guéry and Deleule argue that the capitalist interweaving of society and the body creates a historically new and distinctive category, the productive body. They do not mean that this is a body that produces things in general, but one that has been organized to produce commodities and thereby surplus-value, or profit, for the capitalist. "Productive" in this sense should be taken as a mode of labor organization designed to deliver surplus-value through the exchange of wages for a worker's labor-power that results in the production of commodities for sale on the impersonal marketplace. As Marx writes in *Capital*: "Capitalist production is not merely the production of commodities, it is, by its very essence, the production of surplus-value.... The only worker who is productive is one who produces surplus-value for the capitalist.... To be a productive worker is therefore not a piece of luck, but a misfortune" (I:644).

Guéry and Deleule argue that capitalism's creation of a "productive body" is made possible by squeezing out the awareness of the social nature of work, the social body, in favor of a sense of an individualized "biological body." The tripartite relationship between the biological, social, and productive is collapsed into a stark binary. The purpose and consequence of this elimination of the "social body" and reduction into binary categories is generally to disconnect individuals from a collective identity that might resist capitalist exploitation, and to develop and enforce a functional division between knowledge (the "head" or "mind") of the production process and labor necessary for its operation (its "body"). "Capital" drives the "migration of productive energies into the capital or *capitulum* of the body, the head" in order to make it seem as if those who "know" by overseeing and supervising the work process are the source of surplus-value, rather than those actually doing the labor. This maneuver makes it seem as if knowledge is not a shared human, collective endeavor, but belongs to a specialized corps of managers. Hence it localizes and privatizes consciousness and the authority it conveys in ways that are hinted at by the etymological derivation of capital from Latin *capitulum* or *caput* ("head").

Guéry and Deleule's claim that a particular phase of capitalism strove to create this split is immediately significant for how it extends what is implicit but not fully unpacked in Marx's critique. First, while students of Marx are familiar with what he called the fetish of the commodity, they are often less aware of how Marx extends this model to cover the overall dynamics of capitalist societies. When capitalists sell commodities on the marketplace, they make it seem as if a commodity creates profit by itself, rather than understanding that the commodity has embedded surplus-value due to the labor-power that has been expended on its production. As the commodity seems to generate profit by itself, it becomes bathed in an aura, much like the supernatural nimbus that religious fetishes are believed to possess. Guéry and Deleule, however, do not focus solely on the commodity-fetish, but rather emphasize that capitalism creates other fetishes as well. One of these is an intellectual-fetish that emerges due to capitalism's organization of the productive body, wherein it seems as if managerial knowledge is the source of profit and that it is the expertise of supervisors that directs the social body in ways that generate its productive or profitable activity. By splitting the social body into the starker binary of biological and productive bodies, capitalists establish a historically unique antagonism that Guéry and Deleule feel has been signaled in *Capital*, but needs to be "re-examined, extended, and taken seriously." This question becomes the focus of Guéry's essay.

The Productive Body then makes make a second important move as it uses the tripartite categories of the biological, social, and productive to propose that the modern notion and experience of human individuality outside the social body should be understood as a feature of the particular tactics that were developed by the capitalist revolution of early modern labor practices and the rise of bourgeois domination. Further, they see this modern division of the mind from the body as predisposing the creation of a field of knowledge that assumes that it can investigate a conceptual object that can be isolated, e.g., the "mind," just as capitalism makes it seem as if a commodity exists above and separated from the proletarian bodies that actually make it. All the "psych" fields (disciplines in the sense of fields of research) are held up as falsely objective insofar as their topic or object of study is itself a construction emerging from historical capitalism. Guéry and Deleule's point here is not that the mind has to exist within the body, as phenomenology would have it, but that the separation (*scission*) of the two is a particular kind of alienation and useful tactic that allows a third presence (a mediator) to intervene and appropriate social control.

This claim sets up *the Productive Body*'s larger rejection of the structural marxism associated with Louis Althusser. Althusser was known throughout the 1960s for proposing a distinction between "science" and "ideology," objective truth-making and deformed claims. A long-standing member of the French Communist Party, he particularly sought to define marxism as a *science*, much like natural science, and to assert that Marx's arguments about historical change could stand as objective models outside of the historical refraction of thought. Today, most western marxists read Marx's claims about the "laws" of capital as indicators of strongly determining tendencies, rather than mechanistic predictions of immutable and inescapable processes. Similarly, decades of cultural studies and critical theory on matters of representation have left Althusser's claims of purified knowledge by the wayside, but this marginality would not have been the case in the early 1970s when he was routinely seen as one of Euro-marxism's leading intellectuals. Guéry and Deleule sidestep this debate ("it matters little...whether psychology is an ideology or a science"), since they want, rather, to examine Althusser from a higher level of critique. They insist that psychology's "discourse and practices are inscribed within a historical 'project,'" i.e. capitalism, which has determined in advance the parameters that allow the debate to occur in the first instance. For Guéry and Deleule, the science/ideology division has not recognized that this separation is itself a residue of capitalist scissoring of the social body. Rather than simply disagree with Althusser, their argument implies that his approach to the problem is inadequate in that he has not acknowledged the historicity of the concepts on which he relies.

While the notion that psychology as a professional discipline has its terms circumscribed by the historical conditions of their use might not initially seem to be a strong reply to Althusser, particularly in the twenty-first century when this point has been widely accepted, Guéry's essay will use this initial claim to set the stage for a larger disagreement about Althusser's model for the construction of subjectivity. In one of his most influential essays, "Ideology and Ideological State Apparatuses: Notes Toward an Investigation" (1971), Althusser argues that ideology is a "representation" of the "Imaginary relationship of individuals to their Real conditions of existence," a phrase that echoes the psychoanalytic terminology of Jacques Lacan and refers to the tension between a prediscursive Imaginary (a category of consciousness in Lacan's threefold model of psychic structures) and actual material existence. Althusser then goes on to assert, "ideology interpellates individuals as subjects" and uses the example of being "hailed" or "called" into a social role or existence, usually by authorities that have the power of "naming." His example is the "most commonplace everyday police (or other) hailing: "Hey, you there!" Hearing this, "the hailed individual will turn round. By this mere one-hundred-and-eighty-degree physical conversion, he becomes a *subject." (Lenin, 174).*

This moment of naming is Althusser's materialist and semiotic version of the Lacanian "mirror stage," in which the fragmented subject identifies with a specular image of its own wholeness or unique individuality, and thereby emerges as a unified ego, albeit in an "imaginary" sense that is a necessary stage on the way to the subject's insertion into a symbolic system anchored in language. Since the conditions, forces, and rules that construct the subject are not of its own making, the subject paradoxically must accept and internalize an external system in order to articulate an internal sense of selfhood.

Althusser's use of Lacan's language-based model to convey how the capitalist State's explicit violence becomes tolerated through the more implicit violence of ideological positioning has been massively influential in post-1960s theory for describing how subjectivity arises through the intersection of social control (to be a subject is to be subjugated, subject to authority) and experiential identity (to be a subject is to have a sense of self, of subjectivity). Even performativity theory, in which subjects demonstrate or re-represent the act of naming and shaming, accepts the wider logic of Althusser's account of identity-formation.

Early in his essay, Guéry introduces Althusser's scene ("the question 'who are you'"), only to turn it on his head and refuse the "Althusserian exegesis." Guéry suggests that the preliminary question is not, how does the individual respond to being hailed, since all this does is put the individual on trial for their own self-identification. Rather, the question we ought to ask is, what is the historical formation of the *institution* that certifies the police officer or others and gives the figure of authority the confidence of her or his power over others? How have certain groups become authorized to ask these interrogatory questions, and why do they customarily enact these questions in order to guard private property?

Thus, Guéry begins with what we might call a matter of reverse interpellation by focusing on the mechanism of the inter-rogating institution and its officers, rather than on the subjected individual. More simply, he suggests that Althusser has submerged the actual matter of class conflict in favor of an individualizing model. In order to understand modern power formulations, we need instead to look first at the capitalist, rather than at the proletarian.

In this way, *The Productive Body* reverses or distances itself from what would become an influential pathway in post-1960s and post-marxist critical theory that has focused on matters of identity rather than class-defined management. Guéry and Deleule's revision of Althusser's model exemplifies the move from understanding subjectivity as emerging from sign-systems, i.e. "language," to a model of "discourses" that analyzes the truth-formations created by institutions and professionals. Yet

Guéry and Deleule do not simply signal the turn from language to discourses; rather, their analysis insists that these discourses must be contextualized within the historical account provided by Marx's *Capital*. This last insistence, we want to argue, is a large part of what makes *The Productive Body* important to read today.

One attraction, then, of returning to *The Productive Body* is to see the fork in the road so that we can go back and look down the path less taken. While *The Productive Body* is not a fully-fledged work and often self-admittedly functions polemically, rather than forensically or conclusively, it opens a path that we can develop further. To best understand this aspect of the book, however, it helps to have an understanding of the historical tale of capitalism's development as Marx provides it in the first volume of *Capital*, for this narrative is fundamental to the book's arguments.

4.

In *Capital* volume I, Marx divides capitalism into three emblematic historical periods, which he calls eras or epochs. He characterizes each era by its dominant form of exploitation: these are the ages of Handicrafts, of Manufacture, and of Large-scale Industry. The era of Handicrafts, or artisan-led guild production, ran in Europe from roughly the late fifteenth to the mid-sixteenth century. This period witnessed the early moments of the transition into capitalism as a social formation that brought together the profits that flow from the break-up of feudalism, the dispossession of agrarian workers, long-distance mercantile trade, and usury. The next phase, the era of Manufacture, ran from the mid-sixteenth to approximately the last third of the eighteenth centuries. The shift from the age of Handicrafts to that of Manufacture is as significant for Marx as the difference from pre- or weakly capitalist societies to more definitively capitalist ones. The latter transformation is often discussed as the "transition" debate about when and how exactly the transition from feudalism to capitalism occurred, but this is a question that *The Productive Body* does not take up, and thus one that does not concern us here.

In the era of Handicrafts, capitalist interests arose but were not yet dominant. The groups that we call the middle-class or bourgeoisie did not yet have the political or economic control they will later acquire. Consequently, these factions had to work with the social formations they encountered, not the ones that they would prefer. During this time, the commodity production process, outside of food, energy, and raw material production, was controlled by urban guilds that limited the number of workers a master could supervise, protected work and pay conditions, and prevented masters of the same trade from clustering workshops near each other in ways that might undercut each other's regional monopolies on services. The initial capitalists, often themselves artisan masters, had to accept the fundamentals of this system, but they could place pressure on the existing work structures to produce greater profit. The main way they achieved this was simply by making laborers work longer hours for the same pay. Work procedures did not fundamentally change; the working day was simply prolonged.

In the ensuing phases of Manufacture and Large-scale Industry, capitalists began to get "inside" the work process by eroding guild protections over labor conditions. Marx calls this shift from the first phase of capitalism to the next the move from the production of *absolute* surplus-value to that of *relative* surplus-value. The difference between absolute and relative is that the first is able to transform the work process only from the outside (it prolongs the working day, but cannot change the essentials of the work process), while the second actually rearranges the internal composition and manner of work. Marx calls the latter "relative" because it alters relations of labor within the production process.

Unlike the era of absolute value production (corresponding to the era of Handicraft production), relative value production informs two eras. The first is that of Manufacture. Marx highlights two paradoxical features that occur in this period. The first involves what he calls cooperation. Previously, in the Handicraft system, artisan workers or their suppliers often worked in small groups and in separate buildings, for example cottages and small workshops. Masters oversaw a limited number of apprentices and journeyman in their workshops, or families worked in isolation to do basic tasks such as weaving or carding. Now, in the era of Manufacture, capitalists begin to achieve profit through economies of scale. They bring together or conglomerate workers within larger organized spaces called manufactories, or more simply, factories. This clustering provides more profit to capitalists since it is cheaper to house workers in one large space than in multiple smaller ones, and many efficiencies are achieved by organizing production activities in a single space. Additionally, by working in groups or co-operating with one another, laborers tend to encourage each other to work faster and harder. Because humans are social creatures, we tend to restore each other's energy and increase our work-efficiency when surrounded by others.

Yet as workers are brought together, they are also broken down. Previously a worker was trained with knowledge of the entire process of producing an object. A cooper, for example, would learn all the steps involved in the creation of barrels, or a cobbler all the aspects involved in the manufacture of a shoe. In the age of Manufacture, however, the work process is broken down into smaller constituent parts, so that a laborer learns and executes only one part or moment of the production process, over and over again. Rather than having one worker carry out many production tasks, which is inefficient and loses time as the worker puts down and picks up different tools and so on, a commodity now moves through space while being transferred through different hands, each of which completes a single, unique operation. Additionally, each worker is now equipped with newly invented tools to help them complete their single operation, rather than less specialized tools that carry out a variety of tasks.

As laborers know fewer aspects of the work process and lose familiarity with the overall system of manufacture, they become "specialized" or "detail" workers. The invention of many new instruments also tends to deskill laborers, since inevitably it seems that the tool, rather than the worker, is what does the work of that segment. In a dialectical fashion, the age of Manufacture creates a new social body, a collective worker who now must labor in groups and is dependent on others in a trail or chain of production, since each laborer only accomplishes a fraction of the commodity's total creation. This fragmentation, or parcel-lization, of the work process helps the master craftsman overcome the former power of the guilds, since it destroys the control of knowledge over a commodity's production that workers still possessed in the previous stage. And as workers need only learn a single aspect of the work process, it becomes easier to train larger numbers of laborers quickly and easily.

By increasing the number of potential laborers and fragmenting their labor in this manner, capitalists can set workers against one another. As workers become easier to hire and fire, they are increasingly compelled to compete against one another and to consent to work for less money than others. This competition makes it seem to workers that they do not belong to a class or "social body," but must rely on their individual self or "biological body." Hence the "productive body" that has been created initially in the factory makes the biological body seem more important than the social body. As the work process becomes segmented, structural forces lead workers to begin to see themselves in terms of individual rather than group interests and demands.

If Manufacture began the process of de-skilling workers by

separating them from knowledge of the whole commodity's creation, then Large-scale Industry, the next phase of capitalism, intensifies this segmentation by amplifying the division of labor between the mental and the manual. The introduction of large-scale machinery in the factory shifts the balance of power even further toward the capitalist. In this era, which was Marx's, the manufacture of commodities becomes industrialized so that production is done less by many workers handling *tools*, than by fewer workers *watching* machines that mechanically combine what previously had been separated. Whereas earlier tools were invented to mirror the actions of the human body, large-scale machinery forces humans to adapt their posture and even their conception of their own body's capabilities to the machine's operations. Humans become subordinated to industrial machinery in ways that make it appear as if the machines are making the commodities, while the humans are mere passive accessories.

Marx defines machinery in a manner that initially may appear puzzling or counter-intuitive. A machine for Marx has three aspects: (1) a source of motor movement, what he calls a "motive power"; (2) a "tool" or working apparatus; and (3) a "transmitting mechanism" (*Capital* I: 494). It is irrelevant, on this analysis, whether a machine's motive power is human or animal force, coal, gas, or electricity. Further, a machine is not defined as a complex tool. Instead, what makes a mechanism a machine is the "transmitting mechanism," the aspects of the apparatus that link different tools together. Thus Marx defines a machine less by its parts or immediate functions and goals, than as a new system of coordination. By transferring power from a source to other parts of the apparatus, a machine allows objects to co-operate in ways that humans previously did in the age of Manufacture. While the age of Manufacture fragmented the work process and diminished workers' cognitive understanding of the whole process, the arrival of automation vastly increases human marginality as it turns laborers into spectators of the industrial process who are barely aware, not only of how a whole commodity is made, but indeed of how any part at all of the process actually occurs, and lack any sure sense of the system's boundaries. As workers are increasingly made ignorant of the mechanisms that replace them, a new stratum of observers arrives and is entrusted with the knowledge of how to coordinate operations. These new observers and coordinators are the non-manual engineers and managers, who function as intermediaries between the workers and the capitalists. Consequently, the era of Large-scale Industry creates and brings with it a new, modern division of labor between what used to be called, in the US, white-collar professional-managers and blue-collar manual or service laborers.

In the published version of *Capital*, Marx separates the era of Handicrafts, an earlier stage of capitalism dependent on the creation of absolute surplus-value, from the later eras of Manufacture and Large-scale Industry, phases dominated by relative surplus-value. Another useful distinction, however, appears in a long section that Marx originally intended to include in *Capital*, but ultimately did not. Entitled "Results of the Immediate Process of Production," this section received relatively little attention when it was initially published (in German and Russian) in 1933, at the time Hitler was seizing governmental power. Overlooked during a moment that had more pressing concerns, this lesser-known section was reprinted during the late 1960s in other European languages and began to attract wider notice. One significant element of this additional text, from our perspective here, is that some of the terminology Marx adds in this section is important for understanding *The Productive Body* (see note 61).

In the "Results" passage, Marx discusses the ways in which capitalism appropriates, incorporates, and revises pre-capitalist social features. He calls this process the "subsumption" of labor under capital, and uses it to describe how capitalism subsumes or incorporates and transforms earlier social forms. Marx distinguishes two types of capitalist subsumption, calling them "formal" and "real," and correlates them with the differences between periods dominated by absolute and relative surplus-value: "formal subsumption" occurs in the period of absolute surplus-value, while "real subsumption" accompanies relative surplus-value. Formal subsumption takes place when capital "takes over an *existing labor process* developed by different and more archaic modes of production...an *available, established labor process*. For example, handicraft, a mode of agriculture corresponding to a small, independent peasant economy" (I:1021). In this case, "work may become more intensive, its duration may be extended, it may become more continuous or orderly under the eye of the interested capitalist, but in themselves these changes do not affect the character of the actual labor process, the actual mode of working" (I:1021).

This *"formal subsumption of labor under capital"* involves "the takeover by capital of a mode of labor developed before the emergence of capitalist relations"; in other words, pre-existing economic relations continue even as they are replaced with new forms of sociopolitical organization. The historical onset of formal subsumption, however, does introduce a new *"mode of compulsion"* that is no longer "based on personal relations of domination and dependency," (I:1021) such as feudal relations in which lord and serf mutually recognize their respective privileges and responsibilities. This period is *"formally* distinct from earlier modes of production" because "all that changes is that compulsion is applied, i.e. the method by which surplus labor is extorted" (I:1025). Thus "the labor process goes on before" while the feudal relations of "domination and dependency" (*Herrschaft-und Abhängigkeitsverhältnissen*) are replaced with a new form of "supremacy and subordination" (*Über- und Unterordnung;* I:1026). This new form of subordination replaces feudal social relations with primarily economic relationships defined by the impersonal marketplace, especially as serfs are "freed" from the land and forced to commodify their labor in the wage market-place. Thus, while *"technologically speaking,* the *labor process* goes on as before," the forms and conventions of work-limits are changed as a result of this process of "formal subsumption" (I:1026). Intriguingly, Marx here suggests that economic class interests alter social, political, and cultural forms *before* they can transform the actual economic mode of production.

In contrast to formal subsumption's linkage to absolute surplus-value, Marx describes an ensuing phase of *real subsumption* that corresponds to "the production of relative surplus-value" in which "the entire real form of production is altered and a *specifically capitalist form of production* comes into being (at the technological level too)" (I:1024). This turn trans-forms the "corresponding *relations of production* between the various agents of production, and above all between the capitalist and the wage-laborer" (I:1024). Through the use of cooperation, segmentation of labor, and machinery, the process of real subsumption begins to "take over all *branches of industry* not yet acquired" by capitalists (I:1036). Consequently, real subsumption creates new "productive forces of direct social, *socialized* (i.e. collective) labor" and "the transformation of production by the conscious *use* of the sciences, of mechanics, chemistry, etc. for specific ends, technology, etc. and similarly, through the enormous use of *scale* corresponding to such devel-opments" (I:1024). This transformation exemplifies an inter-relation between the new use of knowledge to organize human collectivity and the shift from isolated pockets of capitalist *activity* to an integrated capitalist *world-system*.

Marx's linkages of the eras of absolute surplus-value with formal subsumption and of relative surplus-value with real subsumption may initially seem merely an exercise in termi-nology. Given the similarities between the descriptions of absolute surplus-value and formal subsumption, why, one may well ask, does Marx develop a new term and set of distinctions and then, by removing these pages from the final version of *Capital*, volume I, decide not to use them? One reason for the excision might be that, in the "Results," he seems interested in raising the question, beyond simply describing shifts in techniques for generating surplus-value through the production process, of how capitalism changes social relationships. Possibly he felt that introducing this broader commentary on social affairs or social transformations clouded his line of argument in *Capital* volume I, which focuses on the production process of capital. Nevertheless, for those interested in understanding and responding to the globalized spread of capitalism in the twentieth and twenty-first centuries, in moments that Marx did not live to see, this rediscovered material opens a new window for analysis of the alterations of knowable social relations by, and in favor of, capitalist forces.

This discussion has three major implications for the arguments of *The Productive Body*. First, Marx's distinction between the era of Handicrafts (absolute surplus-value) and those of Manufacture and Large-scale Industry (relative surplus-value) raises the question as to when capitalism began. Is this beginning to be located in the fifteenth, or rather in the eighteenth century? Elsewhere, in the published versions of *Capital*, Marx more consistently opts for the earlier date. The "Results," however, emphasizes the later date, and this may also have been a factor in the decision not to publish the section. Interestingly, Guéry and Deleule, place their focus on the later date, since their claim about the rise of the productive body rests on the implications of supervision by knowledge and the machinification of society during the relative/real phase.

Second, the "Results" clarify a possible confusion over the keyword "real." Guéry and Deleule use "real" to suggest the changes associated with real subsumption, that is, a new phase of historical capitalism that emerges at a particular historical juncture. Much left critical theory after the 1960s has become accustomed, however, to hear the term "real" as an allusion to the Lacanian triptych of Real, Symbolic, and Imaginary. We need to remind ourselves that Guéry and Deleule employ "real" in the Marxian and not the Lacanian usage, since so much of their intervention is a critique of the manner in which the psycho-disciplines are caught within capitalism's web, and since Lacanian-inflected use of the term often alludes to critiques of foundationalism developed in reference to the "linguistic turn."

Third and finally, Guéry and Deleule's emphasis on the links of science with real subsumption aims to highlight the question of knowledge, rather than the formation of a "collective worker" that Marx also lists as a feature of the period. The concept of the collective worker was taken up and developed by post-war Italian autonomist theory, today most often associated with Antonio Negri. When *The Productive Body* appeared in the Paris of 1972, Negri and Italian neoanarchist theory were not the prominent influence they would later become. For instance, the slogan of the "commons" environmentally hearkens back to earlier discussions of the collective worker. Thus, while it would be a mistake to construe *The Productive Body* as a conscious reply to Negri, we, from our current viewpoint, can see the early 1970s as a moment when distinct emphases branch off from one another; one yearning for new subjectivities based on the collective body, and the other seeking to understand what Guéry and Deleule call the productive body, which develops the implications of the split between managers and laborers. More simply, when read today, we might say that *The Productive Body* is a kind of map of roads not taken, and one that suggests a different direction than that of today's neoanarchists and autonomists.

5.

After their joint foreword, Guéry begins his essay by distinguishing between being productive (a producer), and the faculty of productivity. He does not assert that the human worker is always a "producer," since he sees forms of creation outside the capitalist marketplace. A child transforms materials in play, but not for commercial exchange, even if the resulting object is given or transferred to others. Productivity, on the other hand, is Guéry's term for production shaped or directed by a third party, whom Guéry calls a mediator, one who directs the process of a commodity's production only so that it may be sold for profit. Being a "producer" and being "productive" are two different matters; the first is a general and non-capitalist term, while the second involves working for an alien power to create profit. Guéry's distinction echoes Marx's notion that to be a productive worker is a bit of misfortune. For Guéry, then, the productive body's essential relationship is not with nature, but with the marketplace.

Guéry's larger concern is to track the move from tools to machines within what Marx called the "real subsumption of labor"; this is the transition from a mode in which technology tries to replicate human physiology by producing many different tools, to one that forces humans to *adapt* to the machinery of Large-scale Industry and its new systems of transmission. Whereas a physician intervenes against morbidity with thera-peutic salves, Marx, the "scholarly physiologist," attempts to discover the malady and trace the creation of a productive body from the damage done to the social body, especially the *corps* of guild crafts corporations, which previously protected the body from the capitalist alienation of labor, the *scission* of the body from its own powers. Here Guéry uses a term sometimes associated with Lacanian psychoanalytic notions of splitting in the production of the subject, but the term is recoded here to mean the alienation inherent in the commodification of labor as labor-power. The particular form of separation that he pursues is the fragmentation of the social body into individuals, in the sense of individualized productive bodies.

28

While the medieval guild *does* machinify the forces of the body and mind, it does not separate them into distinct organisms or fetishize one part in isolation from the other. Because the guilds did not separate management from labor (the guild master was still a worker), they did not attempt to isolate the body from mind. Using Da Vinci's well-known drawing of the human body gathered within a circle to exemplify the integration of body and mind, Guéry maintains that "Incorporated-man," man individualized in his body outside of the guild, loses this relationship. Following Marx, Guéry does not hold that the appropriation of surplus in a hierarchy of labor never existed prior to capitalism, but rather that, as the proto-capitalist mercantile system bore down on the guild, it gave rise to the mediator as a third transmission element between production and consumption. This mediator, in turn, helps create a new "real" that alters the relationship between biological and social physiognomy, leading to the emergence of a "productive body" through the techniques of co-operation, specialization, and machinification. This new productive body becomes normed by statistical and enumerated surveillance as systemic knowledge is separated or split from the individualized laborer. The mediator's direction and organization of knowledge appears as the "powerful will of a being outside" workers, the will of a new god whose divination is enacted by the capitalist's appointed surrogate, or in other words the agency or not-so-invisible hand of the professional-manager.

"Without violence or visible intrusion," the capitalist mediator takes command of the work process by insisting on a virtual norm of ideal efficiency in all parts of the production process. This productive body is imaginary, not because it does not exist but because the cognitive has been imagined as a separate force that can rule over the alienated worker. Here Guéry insists that the attempt by structural marxists to separate science from ideology has made a mistake, since capitalist ideology works not simply through the "wonder" of the commodity fetish, but with and through rationalizing knowledge, the cold calculation of the real. The crucial problematic we need to consider, thus, is less the Althusserian "encounter" of the interpellating cop hailing his target, than the emergence of *knowledge* as a separate and separating realm. We need to look first, not at the "call," but at the *"place of the cause"* and the history of real subsumption that grants the authority to name in the first instance.

As a result of the "intellectual domination of the overall labor process," technology is no longer experienced as enabling and extending human control of the environment, but as further weakening and fragmenting it. Rather than extending an act that originates with the human body, machine technology makes it seem that the human body is always incomplete and inadequate without technology. This reduction and impoverishment of the laborer is only intensified as the influence of machinery extends into the realm of ideation itself, i.e., as the laborer increasingly internalizes the terms imposed by machine technology and its social correlates, and increasingly forms her or his self according to its laws.

Distancing himself from Althusser, Guéry questions the focus on the collective worker. He suggests that the triangular relationship between the collective worker, individual worker, and perfect tool, can be superimposed on the relations between the social body, biological body, and productive body. Consequently, he refuses utopian or metaphysical socialism that would hearken to the collective worker, or in today's parlance, the commons, because to do so would accept the *effects* of capitalism that have isolated the social body from its structural role in relation to the other two elements.

His "corresponding thesis," then, is that we need to reappropriate the power of truth-formations, the power and governance of knowledge and the "epistemocratic," away from the mediating managers, and aim toward an "appropriation of the productive sciences by manual workers." Alluding to the Chinese Cultural Revolution, Guéry highlights the role of "intellectual unemployment" exemplified by university and especially graduate students, and calls for new sciences of production, of the mind, and of relations between those isolated, be they students or workers. Such a coalition would realign workers and students alike into a broader "cohort of the dispossessed." For readers of his essay, most likely the university educated, the task will be to "adopt the perspective of non-history," and take on the viewpoint of the working-class as those always excluded from capitalism's dominant account of human development. Yet rather than assume an easy or even an eventual victory over capitalism, Guéry cautions we must be prepared to fight and lose and fight again, to be "a paradoxical weed that springs furiously from the ground after every attack" so as to force one's opponent "to attack again and again." Abandoning certainties of the left's rise, Guéry encourages us to be ready for struggle over the long haul.

6.

After reading some of *The Productive Body*, one might wonder why Guéry and Deleule introduce the term the productive body, or productive–power (*Kraft*), which often seems to replace labor-power, a word that rarely appears in their text. Given how closely Guéry and Deleule hew to Marx's *Capital*, never hinting they mean to reform or revise it in any detail, their allegiance to this neologism is unexpected. Similarly, why favor the term mediator rather than the likewise absent word, capitalist? This terminology is suited to their arguments because, while *The Productive Body* gives a general overview of capitalism, the authors seek to emphasize the shift from the artisan guild to large-scale industry and foreground the role of specialist knowledge within a rapidly systematizing world. On one hand, the term "productive body" is used to indicate a labor collective and specific sociohistorical formation, rather than what might be misperceived as other, more individualized or "psych"-ologized versions of class conflict, class conflict as the encounter between liberal individuals in the roles of worker and capitalist. Doing so gives up too much ground to classical political economy's mythology that the marketplace is a realm of individual choice and exchange, rather than seeing the production of the "individual" as a historical consequence of social formations and pressures.

Furthermore, Guéry and Deleule use the productive body because they want a term that highlights the mental-manual division that occurs when capitalism reaches a certain point of development, and relates this division to industrial reorganization. Rather than having to develop in the shadow of the old regime, making compacts with the absolutist regime, or working solely within the factory, the moment of large-scale industry is when capitalist competition moves from the marketplace to the workplace and produces an all-enveloping domino-effect, forcing all processes to become industrialized within its tempo and dynamic. This is the point when capitalism presents itself fully as a *system*, rather than an ensemble of newer interests among a mixture of many older ones. One result of workers losing the ability to make an integral commodity during the phase of manufacture's co-operation and segmentation is that their scission from knowledge quickly goes beyond the inability to understand the system within the local industrial space, and expands to involve all other kinds of networks, from the new metropolis to the nation-state and empire.

Consequently, Guéry and Deleule's emphasis on the term mediator serves not to replace the word capitalist, but to examine the role of information managers who insert themselves between workers and owners, to protect the latter from being a visible target. In a sense, too, this is a counter-narrative to Althusser's explanation of the way that ideological institutions, like schools, provide benefit for the State. Guéry and Deleule want to reconnect the relationship of knowledge to the capitalist site of exploitation, the workplace, rather than directly to the State. The use of the term productive body should not be seen as a doctrinal-minded replacement of Marx's language, then, so much as a tactical intervention, locating what the authors see as a focal point of contemporary struggle, arguably in ways that Marx himself did not wholly see, given his own historical horizon in the nineteenth century's far less overwhelming penetration of capitalism into daily life, social space, and structures of selfhood.

7.

Once Guéry establishes the role of the knowledge-manager for controlling laborers, Deleule carries the argument onward to make a claim for how the productive body is developed into new forms of knowledge and consumerism that will enable the onward reproduction of capital for the next cycle of profit. Deleule's essay begins by discounting two phenomenological accounts of an unsocialized body: Husserl's claim for a body that exists before the symbolic expression of early modern science, and Merleau-Ponty's idea that the body and its senses are the foundational horizons of perception. These two strands of phenomenology fall prey to the notion of a mind/body split, which, Deleule explains, is a historical development consequent to Cartesian philosophy, the philosophy of René Descartes and associated thinkers, and the seventeenth-century advent of modern rationalism. Rather than claiming that an untrammelled body exists before modern science, Deleule argues that the modern period saw the emergence of a new, alternative mode of knowing the body; Descartes inaugurates the modern mind-body dualism and exemplifies the claim that the mind's operations can be separated from the body. This division makes the mind a unique object that can, therefore, be made available for "psych" disciplines and managers, and for techniques of supervision in the workplace and daily life. The "emergence of scientific psychology in the nineteenth century" springboards from the modern mind-body dualism, and allows psychological specialists to avoid dealing with human somatics—the living machine—and use newfound "scientific understanding" on a "psychical object" to institute the new object of study within what Deleule calls the body-machine. Deleule's insertion of a hyphen from the "living machine" to the "body-machine" suggest the latter's integration within a new macro-system, much as a human controlling tools can be integrated within large-scale machinery.

Deleule's larger interest in the construction of "psychology as an autonomous science," drawing on earlier history-of-science work by Georges Canguilhem and others, focuses our attention on the functional consequences of new "scientific" knowledges. A major consequence of quantifying and making-rational the body's senses, for example, is that once a "psychical object" is made "explicable, justifiable, predictable and legitimate," it becomes more "efficient, recognizable, and therefore manageable." This management makes the mind more profitable for capitalism through the inculcation of consumerism. Rather than simply saying that capitalism controls our minds, Deleule makes a more supple claim that capitalism makes our minds "productive" for the profit-system via psychologists who will first divide the mind from the body through other kinds of numerical evaluation, and then re-integrate individuals into a larger system of commodity consumption. The mind is subject to the same kinds of division and recombination as the factory process. Today's readers might find this argument similar to Deleuze and Guattari's notion of territorialization and deterritorialization, but we might say that Deleule's argument implies that those terms are unpersuasive in that they are too abstracted from the history of worker exploitation within industrial spaces.

The "conditions of possibility for the production of a certain scientific knowledge [*savoir*]" about the mind arise when the body is no longer copied by technology, but when machinery is conceptualized as a new kind of life itself. This inversion is a consequence of Cartesian divisions, but it is one that allows machinery to do more than simply *replace* humans in the work process. Far more significantly, it allows machinery to re-engineer the very conception of human biological systems as a whole, with the consequence that machinery becomes the leading metaphor for describing the body's operations. The body is no longer understood in pre-modern ways, or in the way we imagine and illustrate anatomy's function. In classical marxism, the machine is considered dead labor, the inanimate repository of labor-power. Deleule suggests, however, that the body-machine is an entirely *different* way of understanding modern life, life in modernity in the age of Large-scale Industry and after. For the process of making a body-machine will use human vitality or force (*puissance*), to create a new kind of power (*pouvoir*), a labor-power that will produce profit.

The larger implication of this turn is that, if biological life is understood through the knowledge of machinery, then it opens the door for life itself (the *bios*) to be subject to conquest by machinic logic, rather than simply the mechanist claims of an early Enlightenment-era materialism. The body-machine is not simply a metaphor or "manner of speaking"; it "takes something from life" but only to advance cybernetic principles as a life-norm, and not simply as the replacement of life. With this turn, Deleule argues that the body-machine helps establish a new kind of existence, a second nature or life referenced by Large-scale Industry. Deleule's claims are thus very close to Foucault's notion of biopower and his argument that the late eighteenth century and nineteenth century saw the transformation of social control from the old regime's repressive power of physical punishment to the modern bourgeois State's desire to manage life, to nurture

35

it, to make it useful for capitalism.

Consequently the worker must not simply face her "dead labor" in technological form when she confronts a machine, but "the living being must become machine." Dissenting from contemporary celebrations of human-machine interfaces, Deleule might say, paraphrasing Marx: to become a cyborg is thing of misfortune.

Deleule then argues that workers develop two sorts of responses to machines. The first is to see the machine as a kind of death, something that sucks their life away. The second is to affirm that the presence of the machine creates competition among workers as they scramble to accept lower wages in order to escape unemployment. As one worker struggles to replace another on the factory floor, they begin to see the machine not as an object that destroys them, but as an object that will help them live by creating the conditions of their employment. This sense of *life through machinery* continues as we begin to feel that we are only really alive when we use machinery and that its use will give us more free time to be alive. A modern sense of "leisure" is thus created, whereby we feel that we have a deeper experience of life's vitality than previously, thanks to technology. This new sense of life will "free" us to consume more of capitalism's commodities, thus creating a feedback loop of profit making. Thus the body-machine leads to the productive body, the body that helps produce surplus-value through the sale of commodities, and a consuming body, in which pleasure and emotions of well-being emerge from capitalist-induced competition and practices shaped around and by it.

The process of creating machinic life through death starts with the creation of an "organology" or knowledge-formation about separable parts or senses of the body, for example touch or sight, in order to gain an arithmetic knowledge of the body. As the body becomes conceived as like a machine through new quantifications of sight, touch, and so on, humans begin to compete against one another in order to do "better' on these scores, as if achieving higher ratings than others might help us escape death and human demise. The creation of numeric evaluations of the body's senses and actions will then be put to use as a model for how to evaluate and manage a much less tangible object, the human mind.

This claim is Deleule's gloss on Marx's General Law of Capitalist Accumulation, which holds that industrialization facilitates unemployment anxieties that result in the laboring class's poverty through wage-reduction and acceptance of ever more precarious conditions of existence. As competition is instilled and normalized through reference to these numbers, it generates an inevitable sense of failure, a "progressive downsizing of the living element." And once humans feel incapable before the machinic ideal, then psychology arises as means of providing some degree of relief from this capitalist-induced anxiety. But for Deleule psychological disciplines are simply palliative measures that use the promise of relief through consumerism as a gesture to prevent the lowest levels of survival from being plumbed. In this way, concern for ensuring the survival of the human apparatus through the individual consumption of food and so on is transferred into the productive consumption of commodities that will return profit back to the capitalist, so that he can begin another round of purchasing labor-power and raw materials.

Here Deleule ends with a more optimistic conclusion that Guéry's enjoinder of incessant struggle. Deleule suggests two demands: firstly, for "living work" or conditions that allow labor to escape the iron-cage of deathly competition; and secondly, "in everyday life... the recognition of alterity", here broadly meant as a way of living other than that provided by consumerist leisure. If Guéry's essay ends with an air of gritty determination to endure in a post-Hegelian fight without end, Deleule's offers the possible rewards of such struggle.

8.

Didier Deleule was invited by Foucault to participate in the closed seminar that ran alongside the public 1979-1980 Collège de France lectures on *The Government of the Living*. Deleule presented a paper on the Scottish Enlightenment, likely due to Foucault's ongoing interest in the history of liberal political economy. The invitation to Deleule, who was not a regular participant in Foucault's seminars, was doubtless related to the latter's appreciation of *The Productive Body*. Yet the welcome to the seminar was not simply a gesture of kindness. For while Foucault did not seek to create a "school" or group of acolytes, he often used his lectures outside France and the research of those invited to speak at his seminars to signal more explicit connections between his work and Marx's.

Foucault exceptionally highlights *The Productive Body* in *Discipline and Punish* because it encapsulates the latter's themes while cementing them within a clearly marxist historical narrative, which, nonetheless, differentiates itself from Althusser and other receptions of Marx in structuralism and poststructuralism. Foucault's arguments about the relationship of knowledge, power, and the subjugation of the lower classes through the invention of seemingly invisible institutional techniques that create individualizing subjectivities needed an alternative to the Althusserian language-based model of interpellation. *The Productive Body* provides a way of relating the history of capitalist phase-changes and subjectivity that does not depend on an individual accepting the hailing of authorities, and that can be articulated with Foucault's concerns with the interplay of discourses, institutions, and managerial surveillance.

Although Foucault is well known for his claims about the "invention" of sexuality and deviance in the modern period, many readers have not fully understood that Foucault's interest was not so much in these themes per se, as in their imbrication with the techniques facilitating the rise of bourgeois rule:

To the extent that these notions of "the bourgeoisie" and "the interests of the bourgeoisie" probably have no content... what we have to realize is precisely that there was no such thing as a bourgeoisie that thought that madness should be excluded or that infantile sexuality had to be repressed; but there were mechanisms to exclude madness and techniques to keep infantile sexuality under surveillance. At a given moment, and for reasons that have to be studied, they generated a certain economic profit, a certain political utility... In other words, the bourgeoisie doesn't give a damn about the mad, but from the nineteenth century onward and subject to certain transformations, the procedures used to exclude the mad produced or generated a political profit, or even a certain economic utility. They consolidated the system and helped it to function as a whole. The bourgeoisie is not interested in the mad, but it is interested in power over the mad; the bourgeoisie is not interested in the sexuality of children, but it is interested in the system of power that controls the sexuality of children. The bourgeoisie does not give a damn about delinquents, or about how they are punished or rehabilitated, as that is of no great economic interest. On the other hand, the set of mechanisms whereby delinquents are controlled, kept track of, punished, and reformed does generate a bourgeois interest that functions within the economico-political system as a whole. (*Society*, 32-33)

Like Guéry and Deleule, Foucault questioned Althusserian claims for scientific knowledges and saw class skirmishes as akin to an ongoing war with different tactical maneuvers rather than a predetermined pathway to proletarian victory. Foucault's interest in *The Productive Body* may well have been due to due to the authors' analysis of the intersection of professional managers, knowledge formation, and tactics of power. Like Guéry's call for a democratization of knowledge, Foucault called for an "insurrection of subjugated knowledges" by which he meant the histories "that have been buried or masked in functional coherences or formal systematizations" and "these knowledges from below...these unqualified or even disqualified knowledges" like those of the psychiatrized, the incarcerated, and all those other "disqualified" to speak to authorities, much like workers in a factory who are not allowed to respond to their manager (*Society*, 7).

Yet it is not simply the similarities of their concerns that may have brought Guéry and Deleule's text to Foucault's attention. More intriguing for Foucault may have been *The Productive Body*'s turn away from Althusser's influential model of subjectivity through language-system interpellation, while also remaining firmly within a marxist framework about the real subsumption of the everyday. Given the dominance of the linguistic turn in post-1960s critical theory and the rise of interest in a counter-position of non-semiotic claims for bodily or emotional affects, not least of which is Deleuze and Guattari's accounts of schizoanalysis, *The Productive Body*'s alternate account of subjectivity formation through machinic capitalism presents a theme and question for analysis that still remains to be explored at length.

For considering the recent rise in digital apparatuses and social networks and their correlation to the most recent phase of capitalism, a key dimension of neoliberalism, the Althusserian model of speech interpellation might not fully explain processes of our control within the virtual informatics space of the internet or wireless "cloud," where no one is there to "hail" or call you out. Guéry and Deleule's notion of the productive body may consequently serve to provide new or better insights into the unfolding of capitalist relations today in ways that even they might not have fully foreseen in the early 1970s. *The Productive Body* certainly helps us retrospectively understand Foucault's conversation with Marx in the time of its publication, but its attraction for us today may ultimately rest in how it helps us better comprehend the machinery of *contemporary* capitalism.

Bibliography and Works Cited

I. *The Productive Body.*

François Guéry and Didier Deleule. *Le corps productif.* Paris: Editions Mâme (Collection "Repères," directed by Gilles Anquetil), 1972.

—. *El cuerpo productivo: teoría del cuerpo en el modo de producción capitalista.* Buenos Aires: Tiempo Contemporaneo, 1975. Unauthorized Spanish translation by Marco Galmarini.

—. "Responses aux questions sur *Le corps productif.*" Unpublished typescript in French. Collections of Philip Barnard and Stephen Shapiro. 2006.

Deleule, Didier. "The Living Machine: Psychology as Organology." In *Zone* 6 (1992), 203-33. Unauthorized and partial English translation by Randall Cherry, of Deleule's Part Two (titled "Body-Machine and Living Machine" in the original).

Guéry, François. "Dialogue pour *Le corps productif.*" Unpublished typescript in French. Collections of Philip Barnard and Stephen Shapiro. 2012.

II. Selected additional writings by François Guéry and Didier Deleule, listed chronologically.

A. François Guéry

"La division du travail entre Ure et Marx (à propos de Michel Henry)." *Revue Philosophique de la France et de l'Etranger* 167.4 (1977), 423-44.

Lou Salomé, génie de la vie. Paris: Editions Calmann-Lévy, 1978. Republished Paris: Editions des femmes, 2007.

La société industrielle et ses ennemis. Paris: Editions Orban, 1989.

Maîtres et protecteurs de la nature. Co-edited with Alain Roger.

Seyssel: Editions Champ Vallon, 1991.

Heidegger rediscuté, éditions Descartes et Cie, 1995

Descartes: Discours de la méthode. Commentaires. Paris: Classiques Hachette, 1997.

Nietzsche: Ainsi parla Zarathoustra: Traduction de neuf chapitres du 2ème livre, commentaires. Paris: Ellipses, 1999.

Marx: Critique de la philosophie de l'État de Hegel, traduction partielle et commentaires. Paris: Ellipses, 2000

La politique de précaution, dialogue avec Corinne Lepage. Paris: PUF (Presses Universitaires de France), 2001.

Haine et destruction. Paris: Editions Ellipses, 2002.

—François Guéry has also published numerous French translations with commentary of texts by Marx and Nietzsche.

B. Didier Deleule

La Psychologie, mythe scientifique, Paris: Editions Robert Laffont (Collection Libertés, 81), 1969. Italian translation 1971; Spanish translation 1972.

"Psychologie pure et psychologie appliquée" and "Rapports établis et requis entre psychologie et philosophie." In Denis Huisman and Jean Delay, eds., *Encyclopédie de la Psychologie*, volume 1: *Psychologie générale*. Paris: Editions Nathan, 1971.

Hume et la naissance du libéralisme économique, Paris: Aubier (Collection Analyse et Raisons), 1979. Italian translation 1986.

Le commentaire de textes de philosophie, ABC DEUG et PREPAS. Paris: Nathan, 1990 (co-authored with François Guery and Pierre Osmo). Spanish translation 1990.

"L'héritage intellectuel de Foucault: Réponses aux questions posées par Francesco Paolo Adorno." *Cités* 2 (PUF or Presses Universitaires de France, 2000). Russian translation 2001.

Le Football: Que nous apprend-il de notre vie sociale? Paris: Gallimard (Collection Chouette penser), 2008. Illustrations by Lionel Koechlin.

Francis Bacon et la réforme du savoir. Paris: Editions Hermann, 2010.

La Naissance de la sociologie. Forthcoming, Paris: PUF (Presses Universitaires de France).

—Didier Deleule has also published numerous French translations with commentary of texts by Adam Smith, David Hume, Francis Bacon, and George Berkeley.

See also: *Comment peut-on être sceptique? Hommage à Didier Deleule. Etudes réunis par Michèle Cohen-Halimi et Hélène l'Heuillet.* Paris: Honoré Champion (Collection Dix-huitième Siècle, 141), 2010.

III. Selected Bibliography for *The Productive Body*.

Althusser, Louis. *Lenin and Philosophy*. English translation by Ben Brewster. London: NLB, 1971.

Althusser, Louis and Étienne Balibar. *Reading Capital*. English translation by Ben Brewster. New York: NLB, 1970.

Deleuze, Gilles and Félix Guattari. *Anti-Oedipus: Capitalism and Schizophrenia*. English translation by Robert Hurley. New York: Viking, 1977.

—. *A Thousand Plateaus: Capitalism and Schizophrenia*. English translation by Brian Massumi. Minneapolis: U Minnesota P, 1987.

Foucault, Michel. *Discipline and Punish: The Birth of the Prison*. English translation by Alan Sheridan. New York: Pantheon, 1977.

—. *The History of Sexuality: Volume I*. New York: Pantheon, 1978.

—. *Essential Works of Foucault, 1954-1984*. 3 volumes. Ed. Paul Rabinow. London: Penguin, 2000-02.

—. *Dits et Ècrits: 1954-1988*. 4 volumes. Eds. Daniel Defert and François Ewald. Paris: Gallimard, 1994.

—. *"Society Must Be Defended": Lectures at the Collège de France,*

1975-1976. English translation by Graham Burchell. Basingstoke: Palgrave Macmillan, 2007.

Marx, Karl. *Capital: Volume I*. English translation by Ben Fowkes. New York: Vintage, 1977.

Schwan, Anne and Stephen Shapiro. *How to Read Foucault's Discipline and Punish*. London: Pluto, 2011.

Shapiro, Stephen. *How to Read Marx's Capital*. London: Pluto, 2008.

Virno, Paul and Michael Hardt, ed. *Radical Thought in Italy: A Potential Politics*. Minneapolis: U of Minnesota P, 1996.

IV. Context of May 1968 and French Maoism.

Bourg, Julien. "The Red Guards of Paris: French Student Maoism of the 1960s." *History of European Ideas* 31 (2005), 472-90.

—. *From Revolution to Ethics: May 1968 and Contemporary French Thought*. Montreal: McGill-Queens UP, 2007.

Dosse, François. *History of Structuralism*. 2 volumes. Translated by Deborah Glassman. Minneapolis: U of Minnesota P, 1997; originally published 1991-92).

Fields, Belden. "French Maoism." *Social Text* 9/10 (1984), 148-77.

Feenberg, Alan. *When Poetry Ruled the Streets: The French May Events of 1968*. Albany: SUNY Press, 2001.

Foucault, Michel. "On Popular Justice: a Discussion with Maoists." Translated by John Mepham. In Michel Foucault, *Power/Knowledge: Selected Interviews and Other Writings, 1972-1977*, 1-36. Colin Gordon, ed. New York: Random House, 1980 (originally published 1972).

Horn, Gerd-Rainer. *The Spirit of '68: Rebellion in Western Europe and North America, 1956-1976*. Oxford: Oxford University Press, 2008.

Quattrochi, Angelo and Tom Nairn. *The Beginning of the End: France, May 1968, What Happened, Why it Happened*. London: Verso, 1998.

Seldman, Michael. *The Imaginary Revolution: Parisian Students and Workers in 1968*. New York: Berghahn, 2004.

Singer, Daniel. *Prelude to Revolution: France in May 1968*. New York. Hill and Wang, 1970.

A Note on the Text and Translation

Since the first and only French edition of the *The Productive Body* was published in 1972 (Paris: Editions Mâme), two unauthorized translations have appeared: a Spanish translation in 1975, and a partial English translation of Part Two only (Deleule's essay) in 1992 (See Selected Bibliography and Works Cited). The present English edition is a complete re-translation of the original text that strives for accuracy in the rendering of the book's technical vocabularies drawn from marxism, scientific psychology, phenomenology, and philosophy more widely. Our translation is made from Didier Deleule's copy of the French edition, and takes account of its marginal indications of a small number of corrections or additions to the 1972 Mâme text, e.g., an added sentence in footnote 73 on Taylorism. The editors thank Didier Deleule and François Guéry for their generosity in responding to our many questions on the text and its development in the context of their engagements in the 1960s and 1970s.

Translators' footnotes are identified with "Tr. note." Since terminological accuracy and rigor in noting it are essential in rendering *The Productive Body*'s arguments, the translation uses square brackets to alert readers to passages in which a single French term requires two or more distinct English terms, e.g., in Guéry's uses of *parcellaire* and *parcellarisation* to discuss aspects of the division, segmentation, or differentiation of the labor process. Likewise, it uses brackets to alert readers to important usages and distinctions that in English are collapsed into a single term — e.g. the distinction between knowledge as *savoir* and knowledge as *connaissance*, or between power as *pouvoir* and power as *puissance* — and to provide clarifying details concerning a few bibliographical references.

Finally, standard existing English versions of cited texts have been used when available (e.g. *Capital*, volume I), although we have indicated "Tr. modified" or added a footnote when these versions have been altered to bring out differences between Guéry and Deleule's citations and existing English versions (e.g., footnote 80).

Acknowledgments

We thank François Guéry and Didier Deleule for their generous support and detailed responses to our questions on the context and circumstances of the book's initial publication. Fredric Jameson gave early encouragement, for which we are indebted.

We would like to dedicate this book to Neil Lazarus, Alain Kirili, and Ariane Lopez-Huici.

The Productive Body

Foreword

If all production requires means, and if instruments figure among these means, the production by men and women of their very means of survival seems to make their own bodies into the privileged instrument from which all developed technology, including machines, may be derived. All production is social, according to Marx, and thus the socialization of the body is one with its conversion into a means of production. Historical societies did not immediately socialize the labor-power hidden within the biological body, however; this occurred only in a recent past which is our own. This is a task that capitalism is still accomplishing, as it incorporates the biological body into the social body through the mediation of a third body, *the productive body*, which has gone unnoticed until now because it was objectively fetal and indistinct. But far from drawing the biological body toward a state of socialization in which the social body would contain it as its element, the work of this mediation only results in hypertrophy of the intermediary body and slows down this fusion, or even reverses the tendency toward it insofar as the intended socialization is replaced by a privatization of social functions. If a body is defined by its divisions as much as by its unity, it is not the social division of labor, affecting the social body, which performs objectively identifiable formative and repressive tasks on the biological body. It is technical division, inheriting the divisions of manufacture, which operates on the productive body. This division does not simply fragment the biological body; it tears it apart by separating it from its own powers and turning the powers of its own head, as a concentration and summary of it, against itself. Capital is still driving the migration of productive energies into the capital or *capitulum* of the body, the head, and thereby fully living up to its name.

The hierarchized embedding of these three bodies is therefore unstable: the mediating part is subjected to a bipolar translation that is also a productive becoming of all its components. Curiously, contemporary epistemology, including that of the social sciences and historical materialism in its best-known forms, has announced the effacement of production in repro- duction and declares that all productive structures are therefore reproductive. In the domain of life sciences, for example, Jacob's *The Logic of Life*[1] makes reproduction both the criterion of life and the logically prior phenomenon to which the production of each individual is secondary, a mere cog in a larger machine. The autoproductive and reproductive power of social structures is affirmed in analyses in which the play of the most diverse social functions is assimilated to mechanisms of reproduction, so as to confirm a thesis about the accelerated socialization of the two dominated bodies. Schools, prisons, hospitals, unions and parties, in this argument, would rival the apparatus of the centralized State, all working to more effectively socialize, or, in other words, to more effectively break, the biological body. In reality, the tendency is rather toward the privatization of these organs, toward their integration within the productive body as elements of production, or toward the conversion of human material into productive-form. Thus the productive body's formation is certainly induced, in the biological sense of the term, from above by the social body, once the bourgeoisie has invested it with the essential organs (which also allows us to begin to see that absolute monarchy is a bourgeois form of the State). But subsequently this body takes on an ever-increasing autonomy and importance. It is through this autonomy that it marks its submission to the social body and little by little inherits the latter's powers. And thus it is that reproduction (belonging to the hierarchically dominant body that absorbs the two others) does the work of production. In this light, Marx's analyses of the productive body or organism in Part Four of *Capital*, volume I, need to re-examined, extended, and taken seriously. This will be our object in Part One of this work.

If the social body must delegate more and more of its powers to the productive body, then similarly the biological body's autonomy is required at the heart of the individualized productive body. In fact, the status of being a mere cogwheel conferred on the former by the latter demands, in many ways, a certain type of separation that we will need to analyze. This separation—which signals the return of life in a dominated form—in turn necessitates the development of a specific discipline that must seek its own problematic autonomy. The psychology that aspires to scientificity therefore comes to fill a space that was, so to speak, *reserved for it* in the ideological realm, but whose fulfillment is implied only by the real conditions of development in the mode of production. The discipline of psychology, considered here as a "symptom" of the point of expansion around which the field of the social sciences organizes itself, therefore constitutes, at its own level, one of the necessary mediations between the productive body and the biological body: the biological body produced as an autonomous body trapped in the workings of the productive body in its machinified representation. It enters the circuit of reproduction as an element of the productive body, itself subordinated to the social body. But because this basic element is irreducible, in a certain manner, to a general discourse on production, its treatment leads to the development of a particular discourse that alone is authorized to effectuate the necessary mediation. On this basis it becomes possible to understand that, as an element of simple reproduction, psychology intervenes on the surface of the social body, but only insofar as its mediation is displaced, for in the last instance it is the social body that directs the fusion of production and reproduction.

At this level, therefore, it becomes a matter—beyond the tears of the humanist objections that spring up everywhere in the "critical" literature of the social sciences, but also with a suspicion about sharp distinctions of the science/ideology variety, all of whose efforts are dedicated to *thinking* each science's conditions of scientificity (in this instance those of the social sciences)—of reinserting the subject matter of these social sciences (psychology, in this case) back into the heart of the productive circuit in which they assume their characteristic function—notwithstanding the reformist impulses that sometimes haunt them—in the same manner as, but in another register than, the natural sciences. It matters little in this sense whether psychology is an ideology or a science (in fact the problem of science as a superstructure or as an autonomous domain regulated by the laws of thought is considerably changed if, as a productive force, science is localized

in what one calls the infrastructure, in this instance identifiable as the productive body)—and above all it matters little that one hears a constant hue and cry about the completely-autonomous-status-of-the-discipline-that-nonetheless-maintains-close-relations-to-the-other-social-sciences-in-order-to-promote-a-salutary-interdisciplinarity—since its discourse and practices are inscribed within a historical "project" that assigns the psychologist to a space that he only sometimes escapes through the exercise of a "guilty conscience."

D. Deleule—F. Guéry

N.B. Given the limits imposed on us, it goes without saying that we have merely alluded to themes that deserve separate treatment in their own right but that exceed the scope of this study.

Part One

François Guéry

The Individualization
of the Productive Body

Chapter I

Body, Production, Productivity

Spinoza said: we don't know what a body can do. The question of a body's *power* [*pouvoir*] pushes aside another question that we tend to ask right away: the question about what it is, its nature, its identity. We need to know what it can do, before we can worry about what it is. There's still more to this, because the two questions belong to different registers or orders of questioning. The question about power refers to an experience of perception about intensity, an experience of knowledge [*connaissance*] that is direct and without words. Conversely, the question about identity presupposes nomination, and it also presupposes that the body has already been *subjected to the trial of self-identification*. What response to the question "Who are you?" can we expect from someone who has never asked themselves this question? With language, we enter a labyrinth, for we only identify that which has already identified itself with something other than itself. And what does the body identify itself with? The question becomes an enquiry. There's no way out, but we can't avoid it either. Nevertheless, we can refer the question back to itself by asking another: who is it that wants to ask "Who is there?"; who is it that demands that this unknown presence declare its identity?

The answer comes to us immediately: guards and the police. The guards in apartment buildings, warehouses, barracks, in all public or private property. The question of identity is suspicious, because it doesn't know and fears not knowing, because it guesses and fears guessing. The one who asks *who* obviously lacks peace of mind; he has something to lose, and something to hide as well, and something to fear, *a priori*, from whoever may appear. Identity is, in effect, a relation to anonymity. Only the

57

unknown, the undifferentiated, the anonymous have need of a name and number. That anyone at all, whoever it may be, may be unknown and therefore threatening is the reality, the universe, of the one who guards property.

On the other hand, the policial conception of history belongs to those who dominate it. It is the reigning perspective and in this manner the productive body had to deal with the question of identity. It needed a name. Like every unknown, it threatens property, as if it were an empowered form of property. And the name that it bears refers back to the policial universe in a certain manner that needs to be analyzed.

This body is named productive. How does that constitute an identity? Aren't all bodies that way? If we consider the body most generally understood as such, the animal body, we see that it produces, at the least, its own substance, according to the concept of its species. It produces its descendants according to the same concept and we can call it the producer of its species. But we never do that. All the acts of animal bodies are referred to their nature as living beings, not as producers.

Similarly, children have the capacity to transform materials given to them as they play, but in so doing they're only having fun and certainly not producing.

Being productive is therefore not the property of whoever transforms, or informs, a previously furnished material, as the myth of *creativity*, another suspect term, would have it. In truth, being productive is not the property of anyone or anything, whereas products, on the other hand, are indeed the *property* of whoever appropriates them. This means that the term belongs to the vocabulary of a certain type of proprietor, or owner.

In effect, if being productive is being capable of giving way to products, objects of an appropriation, this is because the final form of production, the product, is valued in itself or in a privileged manner. But who wants products, if not a consumer? Who would appropriate for themselves products that are not in any way consumable? Production and productivity are names given by those who consume; they are signs in the discourse of the consumer.

We call it the *productive* body, not the *producer*. The concept and name refer not to production, but to productivity. In German this is called *Productivkraft*; not productive force, but the capacity or faculty of producing. In the same way, the *Urteilskraft* that is the object of Kant's critique is not the power, but the capacity or faculty of judgment. The faculty! Is it therefore facultative, or optional? Is producing therefore facultative, optional, or in some manner contingent? Is it the exercise of a power [*puissance*] that one could just as easily abstain from exercising? Those who work the earth don't feel that their power of cultivation, their productivity, is exercised in an optional or facultative manner. They attribute to the earth itself the attitude of a capricious landowner capable of spontaneous generosity. Magical practices presuppose a faculty or capacity of producing, and therefore of not producing; they presuppose the suspension of this power. But the power is derived from nature or, if one prefers, there is no isolatable and identifiable productive body as long as the social body profits primarily from agricultural work.

This is because the one who works the earth conceives of herself or himself as the consumer of the earth's products rather than as their producer. This is the only sense in which the term productivity, attributed to the earth, can enter into their discourse.

What this means is that, in order for the productive body to be composed of laborers, and not of a vague unity between the earth and those who exploit it, consumption must be socially and not naturally cut off from production. There must be a space that allows the consumer to see production as an alien power [*puissance étrangère*] which functions in the consumer's service and which suspends its power or service. But it's not enough to speak of a space or a distance if we cannot say who it is that separates, that pushes away and occupies the space delimited in this manner. We can assume that the mediator will act in his own self-interest, and will ensure that he maintains considerable power [*puissance*] over the parties placed in relation to one another in this manner.

This mediator is the proprietor of the products. The productive body exists for the consumer; it exists from the consumer's point of view under this name. It therefore exists for and by the consumer's products. To be the proprietor of products is to dominate production.

Whoever appropriates products appropriates their sale, or the *market*.

We see then that the productive body exists only in a market economy or a mercantile mode of production. The secret of the empowering or suspension of production, under the name of productivity, is that production is destined not for direct consumption, a second moment in the cycle, but for the market, for the temporary appropriation of products, for exchange.

Conversely, the appearance of the market, of the regime of exchange, of mercantilism, leads to the crystallization of the productive body, renders it visible, gives it a face and an identity.

This separation and division in the productive body, constitutive of this body, is therefore allied with another external, higher division, a social division: that between the city and the country. In truth, the division between production and consumption, the intervention of exchange and distribution, do not affect the productive body itself in an internal way; they only individualize it. Nevertheless, this first great division affecting the exterior of the productive body is the after-effect of a division within the social body. It sets us on a path: any division affecting the interior of the productive body will always necessarily refer us back to the great social division that provoked it.

The division between production and the product, which is exchangeable and consumable, makes a place for a mediator or intermediary. If it's true that the mediator appropriates production along with the product, then we know who it is that the productive body obeys. This is a precious bit of information, for the nature of the servant will depend on that of the proprietor, or master.

The mediator is the middle [*moyen*] term, and it's also the term that designates a means [*moyen*]: the means by which the productive force or agency produces.[2] The mediator occupies the place of the means of production. If production is cut off from its power [*pouvoir*], because separated from its product, then why would it not also be cut off from its means of production? Once the productive body is individualized, identified with a pure power [*puissance*] to produce, a production that is empowered or suspended, then this immobile power [*puissance*] must be given an agent, a trigger, a means of passing into action. It requires the mediation of a merchant who buys in order to sell, who opens the market, who gives the body an appropriate milieu. What would a body be without metabolism, without exchanges, without consumption and voiding?

Thus the merchant knew how to make the productive body into something *dependent*, something that must beg in order to live. But the pimp, the usurer, the extortionist, the scalper are not masters. The dependent force is not subjugated so easily; it doesn't work in the service of whoever holds it on a leash. For this, something more is necessary: what this requires is the passage of the mediator or the middle [*moyen*] term into the very interior of the body to be subjugated, where it can take possession of the decisive locus of its power. The merchant mode of production has not yet taken over production itself; mercantile relations are not yet one with productive forces.

To put it another way, the mediator must appropriate not the means of production—every mode of production does this even as it leaves the productive body intact, each depending on the other—but the means of *productivity* or the inner springs of production.

The movement by which mercantilism takes over the productive body, as a blank force occupying the empty space separating production from the product, may give the impression of inflating the productive body until it occupies the entire economic sphere, until it is made to swallow the very market that is its crucial milieu. The limit of this conquest is the meeting of the two concepts of the productive body and the economy. Since Lenin, we know that the maximum *spatial* extension of the productive body may be that of the planet itself, since imperialism has effectively covered its entire surface. But we must bear in mind that this inflation is the phenomenal appearance of an internal theft and appropriation of the body's productivity by its means, by the blank and parasitic force that has cut it off from its power [*pouvoir*].

We see that the productive body has a historical becoming (actually, it has already *become*, it has developed and ripened, as one says of a cheese. It has become entirely mercantilized, and the blank force of the mediator has spread its contagion over almost all of its cogs). The relevant question about what it can do now depends in real terms on the policial question of what it is, its identity, on the series of its identifications, a series that develops along with the progressive stages of its internal appropriation.

How can we follow this "progress," this progression of mercantile forces' parasitic relation to productive forces?

Chapter II

The Productive Body in Marx: The Capitalist Appropriation of the Body's Powers

When he begins to study the manner in which *capital* increased relative surplus-value, and therefore diminished the value of labor-power [*force de travail*], Marx has to take a historical detour, a backwards turn that confronts capitalism not with its own elements, but with elements that were integrated into another mode of production. This retrospective movement therefore retraces the rise of the dominant economic system, distinguishing its stages and observing its ravages, following the analysis of the movement of *capital* within its own space, the paths that capital traces out in a domain which has become its own.

If this text, Part Four of volume I ["The Production of Relative Surplus-Value"], follows the progressive process of appropriation or of capitalization of elements drawn up from the previously dominant regime, what it reveals is that capital was obliged to incorporate these elements all over again, to integrate them into a new body, which is the productive body. This body belongs neither to capital nor properly to itself. It is a mediation, and at the limit it will become capital's own body, but in a form that is always failed, always unstable.

Thus we will search in Marx for the identity of the productive body. He speaks of it explicitly, and with an interest that is closer to the spirit of a clinician than to historical speculation. This idea can be supported with several erudite remarks, which for that very reason are not decisive. For example Marx's reading of Saint-Simon, author of a *Social Physiology*. Or his study of *the most recent medical literature*, in order to form a diagnosis of Engel's illness and propose therapies in August 1857, at the moment he was also writing the "General Introduction" to his economic work.

In 1857, Claude Bernard had already elaborated his method of physiological experimentation in lectures that built on the work of Magendie. What all this suggests is simply that that there is no reason to think that Marx was not reasoning like a physician or physiologist. In *Capital*, he follows the study of the "overall mechanism" of manufacture with that of its *body*, the factory; physiology follows anatomy, making sense of anatomy. But more precisely, it is notable that he discusses (quasi) organic or physiological phenomena taking place in the productive body only in terms of diseased phenomena or morbid effects. The difference between the physician and the scholarly physiologist is that, for the former, physiological experimentation is linked to a will to intervene *against* the development of morbid or diseased forms of life. The physician directs his hand, his scalpel, his attention to the place where the sickness is. Marx's study of the physiology of manufacture is nothing if not a series of outraged exclamations, of clear perspectives that constantly inform his analysis of its structures and functioning. Everywhere he looks he finds sickness, torture, and enfeeblement; everywhere manufacture screeches and groans. The productive body appears to Marx as a sick patient, and also as a sickness that attacks and tortures the biological body. This is not merely his way of clarifying details in his text. It manifests a will, a will to intervene, that makes these theoretical analyses into the scalpel, the hand that feels, the eye that scrutinizes and sympathizes: the will to know and to strike.

The eye that scrutinizes, the hand....; we have to wonder what the hand is going to inscribe in this flesh. Poor, martyred body, what prescription will be written for you, who will help you by writing it?

Capital itself is this prescription, written out in a hand "twisted with nervous tics due to a bad liver," written right into the flesh, on the back of *capital*, literally and in every sense, on the back of the productive body which is in fact one with its sickness. The finest prescription in the world, since it's not written for money, but against it!

Truthfully, if the prescription is merely the indication of a remedy, then *Capital* itself provides the natural history of the malady, a report on its stages.

We need to know the background and medical history of the sick patient. And indeed he has one: the productive body is a kind of inheritor or descendent of another body, which doesn't properly belong to any mode of production, which extends back to remotest antiquity, and which has survived all the transformations. This is the trade or guild [*corporation*]. But in fact he is not its descendent, since in this domain there is no filiation. He is a bodily envelope, a body possessed by another, metamorphosized, disfigured, altered in its structure and functioning.

The intrusion of market relations into handicrafts, which had always failed previously, now succeeds because the bourgeoisie is powerful enough to impose itself on this current of history.

To be sure, Marx insists on presenting the medieval guild [*corporation*] as a body [*corps*] in good health, one which is extremely well-defended against aggression on its space, a solid and well-built body. This doesn't imply the idea of a general degeneration that the capitalist mode of production introduces into society, but simply this: that the productive body, in the form of the medieval guild, in the eternal form of a hierarchized craft, solidified into a caste, has suffered the consequences of the dubious progress capitalism has accomplished through a mode of labor exploitation. This reinforces the idea according to which productivity is a notion attached to a *state of scission* of force from itself, of the body from its powers. To increase the productivity of the productive body is to increase its energy potential [*mise en puissance*], its reserve holding, its folding back upon itself; it is to increase its dependence and undermine its integrity. The productive body in its guild form has been bled, corrupted, and tortured. It has reached the completed form of large-scale industry only at the price of the degeneration of each of its vital forces in turn, of a sacrifice of its organs in favor of the organism. But this is not all.

In effect, "to be an organism" is not the property of just any sort of body. In this case, it is only a moment in the development of an individualized productive body, a moment in its *individuation*.

The medieval guild, which is also eternal, or at least ancient, *from antiquity*, is not an organism. It is a body, for it machinifies forces and subjugates them to itself. These are the organic forces of the human body, *including the head*. This is important: man's head is machinified by the guild, but as an organic part of the body. There is no question, therefore, of establishing an internal hierarchy in which the head would be spatially or qualitatively placed at the summit, higher than the force of the hands, lungs, arms, fingers, legs, or feet.

The guild is not an organism, because it machinifies each biological body within its proper spatial and intensive limits; within the limit of the field of its powers [*pouvoirs*], respecting its powers and their spatial reach. The guild has a profound respect for the form of the human body. For is it not the microcosm, corresponding to the macrocosm, the creature bearing witness to the excellence of the creator? The body, extending its limbs to their full limits and in every direction, figures and fills out a sphere. The guild stops there; it makes no attempt to extend the sphere. Leonardo de Vinci, once and for all time, drew and inscribed within a circle the cross of the human body with its radiating energy. In our times, a company that exploits part-time labor, so-called "temp work," has made this drawing its logo. By an undeniable irony, the company's name is *Manpower*. Naturally, incorporated-man [*l'homme incorporé*] is closer to a Dionysus torn to pieces than to a Christ hanging like a rag, sagging downward, with a head heavily gazing at the Earth before leaving it once and for all. From this to seeing the signs of a rupture with Christian anti-humanism, of a Renaissance of pagan, ancient humanism, of the appearance of a modern ethic of worldly domination, there is only one step that we have, as yet, touched on only lightly. If it is true that de Vinci's man-cross is the image of the incorporated body [*le corps incorporé*], of the guild body [*corps en corporation*], then there is no Renaissance of the ancient spirit, but its pure and simple perpetuation, across the centuries and their modes, including their modes of production.

Ancient, pagan, humanist, and what have you: certainly from before its incarnation and redemption, insofar as the Incarnation can also be considered as the divine sanction brought to bear, willingly or by force, on man's body. If this is so, then the Renaissance must be either entirely incompatible with modern ideals, bourgeois ethics, and the work of history that leads to fully-developed capitalism, or else considered as a moment of hypocrisy or the hijacking of the meaning of a certain ancient humanism. For capitalism is the sophisticated and materialized form of the hatred of Man and of his body, much closer to the asceticism and negation of Christianity than to any sort of humanism.

The guild is therefore a body that is healthy, solid, resisting. It takes its solidity from an almost petrified rigidity. Because of "the tendency shown by earlier societies towards making trades hereditary. The trades either become petrified into castes or... *they hardened into guilds*" (emphasis added).[3] Marx draws this idea from Diodorus Siculus on ancient Egypt.

This hardening or rigidity confers a stability that is reinforced from the interior by *laws*.

> The laws of the guilds... deliberately hindered the transformation of the single master into a capitalist, by placing very strict limits on the number of apprentices and journeymen he could employ.[4]

67

This protected stability, this conservatism that still marks the artisan spirit as an inheritor of the Middle Ages, implies a disengagement from mercantilism and the market: "The guilds zealously repelled every encroachment by merchants' capital, the only free form of capital which confronted them."[5] What is preserved in this manner is the coincidence or the *superposition* of the two bodies, the biological and the productive body; a superposition so complete that that the distinction between these two entities can only be made through abstraction. Marx expresses this syncretism in imagistic terms: "the worker and his means of production remained closely united, like the snail with its shell" [480]. He sees in this unity a natural defense against the irruption of market relations in the biological-productive body: "the principal basis of manufacture was absent, namely the autonomy of the means of production, as capital, *vis-à-vis* the worker" [480].

But we have not yet understood the nature of the guild's means of defense against the market, the mercantile mode of production. Once again, let us confront the two systems of forces that will become fused in the productive body.

The market appears to be a milieu, an intermediary space for enacting exchanges. It is therefore a neutral entity, with no autonomous forces or any identity that matters. Why this abstract middle space [*mi-lieu*] between personalized and individualized entities, between the productive entity and the consuming entity? This space that both separates and communicates must be referred to a larger division, a great distancing that is being effectuated elsewhere, above or before (all these expressions designating a change in scale or in *body*): a great division in the social body that induces the crease or fissure between production and consumption. This is the great contemporary division of History, between City and Country and, from the perspective of class, between producers or laborers (the country) and those who are unproductive, who don't labor, who exploit (the city).

The city is the grouping of these mini-despots, their safe-house, to which the surplus of labor in the earth accrues. It is only this withdrawal from the earth that can make the inhabitant of cities a consumer who presupposes a producer, a consumer because he is a non-producer, a consumer who needs a producer so that he can forego producing. This is the way consumption presupposes production: it presupposes it because it permits the consumer himself to forego producing; it is the condition that allows there to be, in the person of the consumer, a *real* separation of consumption and production, such that the latter is not implied.

But the power [*puissance*] of the non-producer does not consist in the force of the State or of arms alone. It tends to become sublimated and concentrated into the related operations of abstraction and universalization. The withdrawal from the earth is an abstraction: it abstracts from the *mixture* made up of the earth and the biological body, using both to construct the productive body, a new and unforeseeable element that belongs to another sphere that will require analysis: a non-producer. All of capital is present in this withdrawal or this abstraction, an abstraction made from man's productivity or lack thereof, an abstraction that begins with an idea of man distinct from his relation to the earth and fusion with the earth.

This abstraction or void created between the concrete—the earth and its human and technical productive body—and the abstract, undifferentiated Man, whether producer or not, has a second moment, a moment of conquest or forceful return. After the withdrawal comes the assault; this is the movement of the Universal. Abstract man will be universal; he will force a unity of the earth and its production, the surface of the great mixed geological-biological-productive body. He will make the powers of production into something abstract, distinct from itself and from his body. This entails a dissociation of the mixed body and a return of each entity thus distinguished back on itself: the body distinguished from what it can do.

This is the strategy adopted by mercantilism against the

guild, renewing the inaugural split between the City and the Country, making the Country the productive force whose production, overproduction, and sacrifices are consumed by the City. Now, on the basis of this first strategy affecting the Social Body, a second and deeper offensive develops, under the surface of this great body: attacking and seizing the productive body; holding it down, separating it from its powers; making it dependent on a Universal which is the General Law of Value, subjugating it to the squalid factory.

The overwhelming success of this onslaught will efface, at the same time as it confirms, the great initial split between the City and the Country. It will displace it while retaining the mysterious spirit of the divorce between the Concrete and the Abstract.

The guild as *reunion* of representatives of the same trade, therefore developing itself on the basis of their departure from the rural community and their disorderly reunion in this abstract place which is the city, can be termed productive in one sense: in effect, in this abstract place it is legitimate to distinguish between production and consumption, and thus to have a market filling the fissure and structurally pre-existing its material production. Nonetheless, can we say that the trade guild produces according to demand, that it subordinates the product to the image that the eventual consumer has of it? The masterpiece to be made is not referred to simple use-value conceived according to the taste and the demands of the one who will make use of it. Its value only coincides with the pure idea, the concept of the made thing. In this sense, production and consumption both refer to an ideal common term, the value in itself of the product. And for this reason, the guild is a producer without being productive. It does not belong to the age of merchant production and must be brought into harmony with it. Manufacture will accomplish this task. It is through an imperceptible, almost *stationary* movement—since the guild appears to remain intact and only undergoes a transformation within its own space—that this pressurization into a productive form will take place. Simple co-operation under the aegis of the holder of capital represents the intrusion of market relations into the sphere of production; and even though these are present only in the form of *orders* [*commande*], in the different senses of this term, and of spatial and temporal concentration, this is sufficient to make all production the setting to work of the inherent productivity of a given body, and not its free play. In this sense the productive body comes down from the most ancient period, since simple co-operation was known to the Egyptians and used, for example, for their great architectural works, or for irrigation or any other task whose scale exceeded the capacity of restricted social communities. But here the fact that the orders emanate not from a holder of surplus, a despot, but from the mediator between production and consumption, a holder of money, tips this form, evanescent and old as the world, into modernity.

The entire movement that will develop on this basis, from simple co-operation in the context of the guild to serial manufacturing, the prelude to Large-scale Industry, is nothing but the exploitation and intensification of the manifest productivity of the medieval guild. The lemon will not be discarded until all its juice has been squeezed out. And first of all, this manner of organizing in a productive form is *ipso facto* a gain in productivity because the simple *gathering* of workers, whether of the same or of different trades, allows the effectuation of works that would have been impossible otherwise.[6]

Paralleling the development of the productivity of labor, the function of the mediator will be transformed in both real and imaginary terms, since the image itself will be the operator through which this function will be metamorphosized.

A first aspect of this development is prehistoric and exists prior to the appearance of the capitalist as such.

In effect, the workshop foreman or the master craftsman of the guilds is in a certain sense the prototype of the capitalist, if it is true that the guild, as unity of the means of production and of labor power, constitutes a primitive form of constant capital. It is only through the capacity to *advance* capital in order to increase the size of the workshops, which properly belongs to the merchant who holds money, that this form will become real capital and the workshop foreman identify himself with the capitalist even as he becomes no more than the unity of the various work processes concentrated in this manner.

This is the interpretation suggested by this formula in Marx: "The class of capitalists are from the first... discharged from the necessity of manual labor" [423, n4, quoting Jones]. In truth, if the capitalist comes from outside the guild, he has dispensed with it already or never took part in it. Marx already asserted that this was the case in *The Poverty of Philosophy*: "It was not even in the bosom of the old guilds that manufacture was born. It was the merchant that became the head of the modern workshop, and not the old guildmaster" [CW, vol. 6, p. 186; chapter II, part 2, "Division of Labor and Machinery"]. Thus the guild is only the *former* body of the trade that is now invested and possessed by the soul of modern manufacture. And this soul is represented by the merchant or the mediator who has become the director or head of the guild.

This is what is revealed by the subsequent evolution of the character. Now, for the first time, we are about to see the *mediator* occupy the *central* space in the productive body he has induced. Marx defines this evolution in this manner:

All directly social or communal labor on a large scale requires... a directing authority, in order... to perform the general functions that have their origin in the *motion of the total productive body*, as distinguished from the motion of its separate organs.... The work of directing, superintending, and *instructing* becomes the function of capital, from the moment that the labor under capital's control becomes co-operative [emphasis added].[7]

This formula clarifies another that precedes it:

> At first, the subjection of labor to capital was only a formal result of the fact that the worker, instead of working for himself, works for, and consequently under, the capitalist. But as soon as there is co-operation among numerous wage-laborers, the command of capital develops into a requirement for carrying on the labor process itself, into *a real condition of production* (emphasis added).[8]

One might think the term *real* is opposed here to the terms "imaginary" or "ideal." But nothing is further from the truth. Reality here corresponds to the image, and the image to reality. On the other hand, to this conception of a *transitory* historical mode of production that has succeeded in imposing itself for contingent reasons, which does not exclude the possibility that all the forms of necessity may be among its constraints, is opposed an *idealist* conception of the absolute and atemporal necessity of such a constraint, of such a mode of production. This is what is expressed by the following *doubled* formula:

> If then, on the one hand, the capitalist mode of production is a historically necessary condition for the transformation of the labor process into a social process, so, on the other hand, this social form of the labor process is a method employed by capital for the more profitable exploitation of labor, by increasing its productive power [453].

This formulation, in its duplicity, refers to the double aspect of both the labor process and the directing function of the capitalist. This point is sufficiently important that we need to cite the text that brings it out in its entirety:

> …the co-operation of wage-laborers is entirely brought about

73

by the capital that employs them. Their unification into one single productive body, and the establishment of a connection between their individual functions, lies outside them. These things are not their own act, but the act of the capital that brings them together and maintains them in that situation. Hence the interconnection between their various labors confronts them, in the realm of ideas, as a plan drawn up by the capitalist, and the unity of their collective body appears to them, practically, as his authority, as the powerful will of a being outside them, who subjects their activity to his purpose.

If capitalist direction is thus twofold in content, owing to the twofold nature of the process of production which has to be directed—on the one hand a co-operative process of production, on the other capital's process of extracting surplus-value—the form of this direction necessarily becomes despotic.[9]

It is therefore true, on a first level, that a *productive* function and an *exploitative and social* function of capitalist direction are super-imposed in a single overdetermined act. This reflects the subjection of the productive body to the social body. But this subjection is simultaneous with this same productive body's emergence into the light of day and in individualized form, so that the aforementioned duplicity can only develop as an external parasitism, a superimposition which is very crude in relation to a second doubling that is infinitely more detailed, precise, and elementary: the doubling that is beginning to take place between the productive body and the biological body it has inhabited up to now, within its proper limits. The disconnecting of these two bodies is the truly fundamental and radical phenomenon induced by the transformation of the social body. It functions in two modes, the real mode and the imaginary mode. But Marx does not oppose these to one another; he situates the latter among the mechanisms that make the former possible.

In the real mode, the co-operation of individual workers in a communal task that is unrealizable on their scale reveals a productive force specific to the productive body. The development or simply the experience of the labor process accomplished by the productive body brings the individual's work back to its truth as it concretely produces the category of average social labor, in the statistical effacement of individual differences in the rhythm and quality of work. Thus, in its limited extension, simple co-operation, the first and fundamental capitalist phenomenon on which the subsequent edifice will be raised, quantifies individual work or gives the work accomplished by the biological body its truth which is at the same time its negation: a statistical and numerical norm that only concerns it insofar as it coalesces with the productive body. The category of labor-power [*force de travail*] only appears in this way, and only in this way will this average and social power [*force*] acquire a value, thereby entering the common ground of market relations. The mediator has already contaminated the individual labor-power of the medieval trade, without violence or visible intrusion, merely by his presence in this simultaneously median and central locus of capitalist command.

But this objective and quasi-necessary phenomenon is doubled by an imaginary one: the isolation of the powers [*pouvoirs*] of labor's productive force, the confrontation between this force and its power in the form of an abstract and individualized image. It is because of this intrusion, because of the way that the social body, the relations of exploitation established at the level of the social body, becomes parasitic on the productive body's first relation to the form from which it is separating (the biological body which heretofore possessed productive powers [*pouvoirs*] by delegation), that "the interconnection between their various labors (those of the wage laborers) confronts them, in the realm of ideas, as a plan drawn up by the capitalist, and (that) the unity of their collective body appears to them, practically, as his authority, as the powerful will of a being outside them, who subjects their activity to his purpose." This appearance is thus a false semblance, an optical illusion. Its victim confuses the productive body, of which he has always been a part, even though he has never perceived it, with the historical force which has appeared fortuitously and from outside the sphere of production, suddenly revealing to him and the body's other parts the very body they make up, which had previously seemed enclosed within the biological body for all eternity. Effectively, at the stage of simple co-operation, which as Marx insists is the beginning of capitalism, it is true that this is simply an appearance and that it is simply false, for the productive body is not capital.

The leftist interpretation[10] is thereby given free rein: the capitalist sleight-of-hand is exposed in *Capital*, which denounces capital's parasitism on the productive body and thus separates them conceptually before practice enters into the picture. From a Spinozan perspective that has been adopted in the Althusserian exegesis, we might respond: this is a simplistic conception of the illusion. Attacking the illusion will accomplish nothing unless we do away with its real basis; rather than overturning the illusion, we need to shift our ground and find where its roots are buried in order to dig them up. But, precisely, this is not how Marx presents things. *In no way* does he oppose appearance or illusion to reality. This refusal only seems odd if we rule out in advance the idea of a dialectical turn, of a *Hegelian* turn in the Marxist presentation of history. If not, then shouldn't we expect that the phenomenon will be the appearance of truth, in fact its prefiguration? And that the illusory phenomenon that identifies the productive body with productive capital will project the productivity of co-operative labor power onto the unity of directing and organizing capital [*capital commandant et commanditaire*], will prefigure this body's future and show the path it will follow. In other words, the mediator occupies the central space, *the place of the cause,* first in ideal form, then in real form with no suggestion of what follows [*et sans aucune solution de continuité*]. No wonder, then, that structuralist interpretation is blind to these texts in which a flirtation with the "Hegelian dialectical turn" becomes a shameless coitus.

If the essence of the dialectic is imaginary appropriation, this proceeds to the point at which the image dispossesses the corresponding reality of itself, if indeed it is true that in order to coincide with its own productivity, this reality requires the internal mediation of a self-image that concretizes its own powers [*pouvoirs*]. The productive body presents the biological body with its truth in the form of an image; the social body does the same with productive body and all three subsist, but chained together in subjugation and hierarchically embedded, as it were, under the domination of a single master: universal capital.

How will this passage from illusion to reality be accomplished? Up to now, "their (the wage-laborers') unification into one single productive body, and the establishment of a connection between their individual functions, lies outside them" in "the capital that brings them together and maintains them in that situation."[11] The mediator has only ideally occupied the place of the cause or of the productive force. In reality, he only serves as an intermediary between the productive body and its products. The next stage will make an incarnation of capital the intermediary between the productive body and its productivity. This incarnation will be part of the real force of capital, whose functions are to gather and surveil works. This will be the person who exercises surveillance, but in a new and technologized form: in the form of an intellectual domination of the overall labor process.

This will be the historical task of manufacture, in accordance with its double origin and in its two forms, heterogeneous and organic manufacture (Part Four, chapter 14). Manufacture *intensifies* the tendency for trades to become specialized, or in other words it pushes the productive body's now-overwhelming occupation of the biological body to the breaking point, thus allowing the mediator to invade the terrain opened up in this manner. Among its other effects, this makes obsolete the Aristotelian thesis according to which technology extends the powers [*pouvoirs*] of the body.[12] Even so, the illusion that supports capital and grants it productive powers continues to depend on this thesis, which allows it to take advantage of the split created between the powers or productivity ascribed to an extended, enlarged biological body, and the real productivity of the productive body which, before the stage of machinism, is only emancipated from the biological body in an imaginary sense, and just enough to ensure that the withdrawal of surplus-value remains imperceptible or inconceivable, although quite real.

We know that manufacture is first of all, chronologically or logically, or in a word phenomenologically, heterogeneous. In the example of carriage manufacture [455-56], it assembles craftsmen from different trades and makes them work by mechanical co-operation toward a single product: the carriage, the final and additive unity of the products of the ironworks, carpentry shop, gilders, etc., that compose it. Such a procedure reveals, no doubt, the pre-existence of the goal or end as a formal cause, or the determination of the idea of the carriage in relation to its produced reality. Nevertheless, the cause, acting from the start and perceptively revealed at the end, is absent during the entire labor process and thus allows its unity and that unity's place-keeper, capitalism, to subsist apart from the process and in a function of mere surveillance. But this is not the case in the example of pin manufacture, a serial type of manufacture [456-57]. In that example, the simple idea plays a similar role as formal cause, but has the particularity of breaking down into subsidiary operations that have no sense on their own, each of which is isolated and requires for its effectuation the effective presence of an active cause during the labor process itself; this is the unified operation in which the partial operations converge in a form which is no longer that of simple surveillance, but now that of an organizing element which regulates the quantity, the rhythm, and the very nature of the work being carried out. This means that the representative of capital, the one who possesses the idea, the *engineer*, now begins to play a necessary technological role he did not yet have at the stages of simple co-operation and of heterogeneous manufacture.

This mutation is both the dislocation of the productive body restrained within the limits of the biological body, and most extreme exploitation of the productivity of the body formed by the medieval trade.

From the perspective of purely manual know-how [*savoir-faire*], which is the only kind the guild is concerned with, since it never dissociates manual and intellectual work, serial manufacture is the most extreme development of the worker's virtuosity at detail work. It gives the worker force, precision, efficacy, rapidity, and confident motion. From this perspective there is nothing miraculous, because any other form of constraint besides the law of profit could obtain a similar increase in productivity. Descartes observed that the luthier had his intelligence in his fingers: from this perspective, the fingers of the luthier, fragmented into the steps of serial manufacture, acquire a kind of genius as they develop a subtlety that is virtually superhuman. This goes along with an ever-increasing mechanization of virtuoso skill, which is to say, precisely, a loss of intelligence, an immiseration. This contradiction reflects a phenomenon which is fundamental, and modern to the highest degree: the explosive expansion of Cartesianism, which is also that of the Aristotelianism that makes technology an extension of the human body.[13] It illustrates the transition from one Cartesianism to another: the body-machine thesis is supplanted by the humanist thesis that makes *knowledge* [*savoir*] (and not know-how) the weapon with which man makes himself "master and possessor of nature," *and firstly of the machine-like nature* of the body in general. This thesis makes Cartesianism the philosophy of machinism, not mechanism. But it understands machinism (to come) according to the model of mechanism (which already exists in the additive form of heterogeneous manufacture, whether in co-operation or the medieval trade). This tension makes Descartes the thinker of mechanism and the ideologue of machinism, at once a reflection of the productive body in its primitive syncretic form and a program for the productive body in its developed capitalist form. To deny the Cartesian system either of these aspects is on the one hand to date it in an overly restrictive manner—like Borkenau in *Der Übergang vom feudalen zum bürgerlichen Weltbild* [The Transition from the Feudal to the Bourgeois World View], and Koyre is right to denounce such a flattening—or on the other to overemphasize the prophetic aspect of its ideology and treat it as a foundational philosophy, and thereby to legitimate, as a non-critical epistemology is tempted to do insofar as it ignores the question of the status of the sciences in the productive body, the contemporary relations of production as the application of universally valid rational norms or applied rationalism. When Marx clarifies the transitional and oppressive character of machinism, this gesture consigns to the camp of bourgeois thinkers all those who see in prophetic Cartesianism the truth that allows one to understand the entire past history of mechanism. In effect, the history of philosophy can be judged as political economy: it is bourgeois "insofar as it views the capitalist order as the absolute and ultimate form of social production, instead of as a historically transient stage of development" ("Postface" to the 2nd German edition of *Capital* [96]). Which means that critique, or science, must judge a social formation from the perspective of its future, in other words its negation.

Friedmann-style humanist protests against the specialization and fragmentation of work [*le travail parcellaire, travail en miettes*], shared by leftist currents inspired by Marcuse, which call for the all-out development of technology, or in other words for an even greater, more pronounced inflation of the productive body, act as if Descartes, the Descartes of the body-machine, correctly described the productive body, or as if machinism were mechanism. They fail to recognize that the segmentation [*parcellarisation*] of the physical body is an anachronistic phenomenon affecting only the pre-modern [*antique*] mixture of the biological and productive bodies. The true great division of the body is not that one. It concerns these two bodies, to be sure, which separate from one another progressively during the period of manufacture. In itself, this fact invalidates all critiques of the specialization of work. But this division depends on another, which takes place at the very core of the biological body: the division between the body, *thereby* reduced to a bit of machinery, and the intellectual forces of production, the head, the brain, whose current status is that of *software* [in English in the original] in computer technology. In the end, phenomenological or psychological theses that insist on the unity of the body and psyche or on the Cartesian substantial union are simply carrying water for the historical work directed against the biological body by the social body as it acts through the productive body and introduces the division of these two elements into the innermost core of the individual. In comparison to Marxian historical critique, this partial and anachronistic critique, this apology for what is, and its myth of lost unity, cannot recognize the results of modern history dominated by capitalism.

Thus we are faced with a "productive mechanism whose organs are men" [457]; manufacture, primarily in the serial form. Let's have a look at the trajectory of the capitalist mediator, in his sensational voyage back to the sources of productivity.

As he takes up positions of command over the entire productive organism, the mediator takes over the central locus where the fragmented body perceives its unity, where it requires a unity in order to make the sum of the segmented labor process into a single production, or the production of a single product. Capital therefore interjects itself between the productive force of the specialized worker and his unitary product, taking the technological form of the work of surveillance and of the unification of tasks. It exists, therefore, between capital and work, a solidarity which is both contingent and contradictory from the social perspective, and necessary and organic from the technological or productive perspective. If capital aims for hegemony over the entire process of production, and everything points to this conclusion, then it needs to appropriate for itself not only the function of unifying the productive body, a mediation between production and product insofar as serial production's type of cooperation allows the whole to subsist over and apart from its separate parts, but also the productive force itself.

The problem is the following: in order to appropriate labor's productive force, it becomes necessary to appropriate either work itself, or the worker. Now, capital cannot make itself into labor without contradicting its principle: the capitalist putting himself to work in order to avoid having to pay for the force of labor makes no historical sense at all; this is a Crusoe fantasy. That leaves the appropriation of the worker; but in a market regime where everything has a price, the biological subsistence of the individual worker is quantified and measured in consumable goods. Slavery or salary all works out the same; the work force has to be nourished and clothed. From capital's point of view, the problem takes the concrete form of the search for ways to increase relative surplus-value. And the solution is the stroke of genius that allowed capitalism to spread its hideous membrane over the entire surface of the globe. To transform work itself, to displace the origin of its productive force as well as the form of its expenditure, is to neither work nor appropriate the worker, but to do without him almost entirely, to dispossess him of the very productivity that made him indispensable. The stage that

82

capital must reach in its work of parasitic appropriation is the complete dissociation of the productive body and the biological body, the displacement outside the biological body of all the productivity it previously contained.

To make this productivity external is to push its characteristic manifestations to a breaking point, to a point where they are completely outside the biological body. These are the two moments that inaugurate machinism: the perfecting of the tools of the parts worker [*travailleur parcellaire*], and the introduction of machine-tools.

Through an unexpected displacement along the sides of a triangle, the productive body will be thrust outside any identifiable biological reference, and outside the Aristotelianism of this same movement.

An important trait of specialized [*parcellaire*] work, which applies to manufacture in general, is the functional development it imposes on the tools of labor. These are subjected to the same specialization, the same "differentiation" ["*parcellarisation*"; see passage on tools, 460-61] as the detail worker himself, as if they were truly part of his anatomy or its extension. In manufacture there is no longer one universal type of pliers; every tool is indispensable for one operation, but useless for all the rest.

As concerns the anatomy of the productive body, the variable play of the whole and the parts in production, at the manufacture stage, consists in the following. The collective worker (CW) takes the first place, since he presides over the overall process and verifies its parts. Second place goes to the individual, parts worker (IW), who serves as a relay for the first. Last is the perfected tool (PT) that serves as an organ for the transformation of raw material into a product. In this manner we can consider the three elements of manufacture as the poles of a triangle that links them in a certain irreversible order and that entails a hiatus, because the tool does not refer back to the collective worker.

It refers back in a certain manner, nevertheless, because the collective worker acts as the unity of the process, reflecting the unity of the *product* to which individual workers contribute only fractions. It is the differentiated [*parcellaire*] tool that , by its specialized form, reflects the analytical unity of a process that is divided into its ultimate constituent parts. The fateful break with a millenary tradition, which also conditions Marx's break with any utopian or metaphysical socialism that would reverse the *course* of history, will consist in eliminating one pole and two sides of the triangle, and in saving only one bilateral relation of the productive body to the organs of operation or differentiated [*parcellaires*] tools. Thus we can no longer use the term "collective worker" for a productive organism whose parts are no longer men but machine parts: the productive body ceases to be a biological metaphor.

This outcome concerning the anatomy of the productive body must now be examined in terms of its conditions of possibility.

It is the solution of a double problem for the capitalist: the problem of the valorization of capital on the one hand, and the political problem of discipline for the productive body on the other, characterized thus:

> Since handicraft skill is the foundation of manufacture, and since the mechanism of manufacture as a whole possesses no objective framework which would be independent of the workers themselves, capital is constantly compelled to wrestle with the insubordination of the workers.[14]

How do we go about getting the worker out of the process of production? This is carried out by means of two expropriations, two transfers of power [*passations de pouvoir*], a double decomposition or dissociation of productive force from work, which up to now had always been syncretically joined.

On the one hand, the worker loses acquired, learned manual virtuosity, which was handed down through tradition and preserved over generations of time: this element was partially transferred to the differentiated tool which accompanies and contributes to the exacerbation of the process of specialization.

$$\text{IW} \longrightarrow \text{PT}$$
expropriation appropriation

But how did the productive body take possession of the perfected tools in order to make them its own executive organs?

To accomplish this, on the other hand, it had to appropriate to itself the *remainder*, or the elements of productivity other than manual or physical dexterity in general. This remainder is not plainly legible because it is hidden by the biological body, by its nature. But we can read it on the body in which these decomposed elements will be reintegrated, on the machinified body of large-scale industry. And here the question must be asked: what is the machine-tool, or the system of machine-tools, the great automaton, composed of?

What its composition reveals is, in effect, this *remainder* of productive elements that were stripped or expropriated from the individual worker so that machinism could become possible. Obviously this does not mean that the truth of the biological body lies in the machinified productive body, but rather that from among its *powers* [*pouvoirs*], only the productive elements were removed, selected, and trained up to the inept virtuosity of the specialized [*parcellaire*] task, and at last moved from the extremities of the body to its exterior, to the tools that extend it, all of which results in a biological body that is left without powers or forces, like an empty envelope, terminally mutilated:

> Manufacture… converts the worker into a crippled monstrosity by furthering the false development of his specialized dexterity and sacrificing a whole world of productive drives and inclinations, just as in the states of La Plata they butcher a whole beast for the sake of his hide or his tallow.[15]

What is the composition of "fully developed machinery"? It "consists of three essentially different parts, the motor mechanism, the transmitting mechanism, and finally the tool or working machine."[16]

The machine-tool or working machine inherits the role of the specialized, differentiated [parcellaire] tool. It is therefore in the first two organs that we must seek the nature of the productive forces of the biological body, through their descendants.

The motor organ, engendering its energy or receiving it from elsewhere, reveals to us that human work can be partly assimilated to the physics of work,[17] to the transformation of energy into motion, to the expenditure of energy. It can be measured, and measuring subsequently reveals that man is not a very satisfactory motor. He is limited, neither supple nor powerful. Yet such a motor constitutes the essential force of human labor, once the specialized [parcellaire] tool is developed to its maximum; hence the example of spinning.[18]

It is in the third organ, a simple intermediary, a modest mediator, that capital discovered and exploited a treasure. It constitutes not only the secret of the transition to capitalist machinism, but the essence of the productivity of the two others.

> The transmitting mechanism, composed of fly-wheels, shafting, cog-wheels, [etc.]… regulates the motion, changes its form where necessary… and transmits it to the working machines [494].

Is the regulation, distribution, and modulation of motion a simple function of transmission, a simple interposition? Or is it, rather, an intervention in the basic process of physical energy expenditure, such that it is subjected to the ends of whoever appropriates the product, of whoever has foreseen, prior to any process of production, both the use and exchangeability of the product? Transmission, incarnated in cog-wheels, fly-wheels, and pulleys, manifests the formal causality of production, the priority of the representation of the product over its effective production. But this time the formal cause is partially identified with the efficient cause: it is not the scissors of the sculptor, but the hand that manipulates them, the descendant of this hand. Initially the mediator took over the space that separates the capture of physical energy (the motor) and its expenditure in automatized form (the organ of operation transformed into machine-tool). He therefore became the means by which the material productive force is transformed into production. But this means is directly related to another that tames material energy and makes it work for its profit, to the intelligent and calculating element that presides over the overall work process and, additionally, acts as the necessary preliminary to any work process at all: the element that *organizes* the productive body [*l'élément du montage du corps productif*] and on whom its functioning depends, that is, the *engineer*. If the element of transmission corresponds, in the anatomy of the productive body, to the powers of the head, to the work of an engineer, of an engineer who has foreseen and constructed regulating mechanisms that allow the adaptation of natural energies to their productive expenditure, then its properties are symptomatically those of intellectual work.

Here we see an immense spatial extension of the transmitting mechanism:

The transmitting mechanism becomes an extensive and complex apparatus [*corps*].[19]

Subsequently a "vast automaton" [502] is created, made up of a combination of working machines:

> Here we have, in the place of the isolated machine, a mechanical monster whose body fills whole factories, and whose demonic power, at first hidden by the slow and measured motions of its gigantic members, finally bursts forth in the fast and feverish whirl of its countless working organs.[20]

The insistence on the gigantism of the vast automaton, while it emphasizes the deficiency of the Aristotelian thesis according to which man uses technology to create artificial limbs, also adds considerable reinforcement to the ancient illusion that made capital, incarnated in now giant instruments of production, the natural or divine assumption underlying all production. This is because this illusion has partly become a reality: the unity of works is really accomplished by capital insofar as it appropriated the intellectual or technical forces of work for itself.

It is in the form of intelligence, then, that capital introduces itself, to the mechanical worker-organ of the vast automaton, as the assumption underlying all production or eminent productive force.

The guild has lived its last. Knowledge has escaped from know-how, which was invented in the repetition of learned motions.

> As machinery, the instrument of labor assumes a material mode of existence which necessitates the replacement of human force by natural forces, and the replacement of the rule of thumb by the conscious application of natural science.[21]

And immediately after:

> Large-scale industry... possesses in the machine system a completely objective organism of production, which confronts

the worker as a pre-existing material condition of his work.[22]

Thus the sciences will play the role of eminent productive forces, presupposed by production, the delegated presence of capital in the process of production.

But we need to pause over the logic of Marx's analysis of the productive body.

At this point the phenomenological exposition undergoes a metamorphosis. Because this logic has been confused with a linear, chronological ordering, Marx's text has now presented us several times with a middle term, a mediation, an intermediary, an element or a moment which is thereafter supposed to assume a privileged place, to acquire a central importance. The capitalist merchant is there from the start, then the one who surveils the co-operative labor process, then the engineer or the intellectual element of production whose importance we have just indicated, who gives rise to the *organization* [*montage*] of the vast automaton or the system of working-machines. Is this the repetition of a single figure? The last element of the series is revealing: the mediator, the element presented phenomenologically as the middle term, is none other than the assumption underlying the process of production. This assumption is not, as the phenomenological order suggests, the material existence of locales and machines prior to the arrival of the workers, the work process, or process of production. This is only an inessential *chronological* feature of the priority of the assumption over the process. It does not affect the "structure" that will reveal its existence through the phenomenal succession of its states, for the productive structure is not the same in manufacture as it is in machinism. Yet the assumption is the same, across the difference of the elements that depend on it. *In reality it is a relation of mastery*, in which the forces mastered are identified with nature, and the mastering forces identified with what could be called the will.

One part of the productive forces enclosed in the biological body appear, at the point when they are supplanted by natural forces in the form of the motor, as natural in themselves. A muscle is a motor, and transforms energy into motion. The subjugated element of organic productive force is assimilated to nature. When it was one with the "superior," intellectual or skilled elements of artisanal productivity, this natural character did not appear; so in effect, it is the subjugation that is the condition of its naturalness. Or else nature is the name the master gives to what he subjugates. In this way all mechanisms manifest the same method of relating will to nature. In effect, mechanism consists in bringing a certain number of elements into relation with one another, according to their nature, such that the result is the accomplishment of the ends of the one who has brought them together; a ruse, no doubt, but only half a ruse,[23] since the elements, in acting out their natural roles, or their roles as nature, have no ends in themselves. Mechanism depends on the organizer's negation [*la negation par le monteur*] of the finality that properly belongs to the organized elements, which signifies their forced reduction to nature considered as inertia or self-identity. The naturalism which is installed in the productive body from the moment the capitalist mediator enters the scene, already aspiring to the role of master, is simply a becoming-subjugated, a becoming that is initially wished for, then sought after, and finally obtained by substitution, when the organism of production whose members are men is exchanged for the vast automaton in which men are only accessories or substitutes for mechanical organs.

Thus the role of the assumption, played initially in an imaginary and subsequently in a real way by the creatures of capital in the process of production, now appears in its truth: it marks the stages of an itinerary which is that of capital itself, as it moves toward the place of the master, and also a sloughing-off. Insofar as the productive body emerges into its individuality, it becomes the body of capital, it furnishes the master with his body, his subjugated organic element, his organism.

Chapter III

An Ongoing Metamorphosis: The Naturalization of the Powers of the Head; or, the Brain's Fragmentation

From which side, internally or externally, do we now reach the limits of the Hegelian dialectical turn? In a single motion, Marx always provides both the exposition or use, and the critique, of his object. What holds for bourgeois political economy also holds for the method, corresponding to the logic, of this economy. Hegelian dialectic is the method of exposition in *Capital*. It is therefore both the instrument and object of critique, insofar as it serves to grasp bourgeois economy in dialectical form, as an imaginary and real process of appropriation.

Let's take Marx's text seriously: it has often been taken literally, or at its word. But extending it is a job that still needs doing.

If Marx limited himself to this analysis of machinism, which reveals the subjugation of the manual worker to the intellectual worker, the task-master and servant of capital, capital's delegated overseer of work, he would eternalize the technocratic or, in a way, "epistemocratic" form toward which developed capitalist societies seem to converge, and this would be the limit of its development. The corresponding thesis is the idea that socialism is basically the affirmation of the appropriation of the productive sciences by manual workers, which short-circuits capital and contains the productive body within itself so that it can do the bidding of a renewed social body. The Cultural Revolution, in its most exemplary implications for capitalist societies, constitutes a draft of an experiment in this direction. But if the productive body is, in general, the subjugated element of capital as master, which presupposes that we never identify capital with any of its

92

particular forms, then it becomes necessary to clarify, as a symptom of the maintenance and renovation of this subjugation, a contemporary tendency, echoing those of Antiquity, toward the naturalization of intellectual work or the powers [*pouvoirs*] of the head (naturalization thus signifying subjugation).

The specialization [*parcellarisation*] of intellectual work is well-developed at this point. The difficulties encountered by capital in determining the value of intellectual work, denounced as a defect of Marxist political economy even by Bernstein's revisionism and by Marginalism, are not insurmountable. The division of intellectual labor, a technical division that deprives all specialized [*parcellaires*] tasks of their meaning, and which concentrates productivity elsewhere, along the entire spectrum that runs from the pure sciences to the most specialized technology, has resulted in the U.S.A. in ever-increasing intellectual unemployment, most spectacularly illustrated by its effects on the holders of the highest degrees. Can anyone doubt that these are the latest avatars of that law of capital which foresees the gradual fall of the general rate of profit? But this means that capital's mastery of the process of production tends to impose this kind of naturalization on the productivity of the entire human species, which is thereby inevitably subject to capitalism's ceaseless search for ways to maximize its rate of profit. Therefore, to call for a return to the stage of the productive body's development that favored the sciences over manual labor, or to protest capitalism's waste of the productive forces contained in science and technology, is just as utopian, idealist, and reactionary as the call, frequently expressed by the right, for a return to the substantial union once incarnated by the medieval guild (Marx attributed this latter tendency to Proudhon). Novelty and the progress of one research domain or scientific practice relative to others are dependent on the search for the maximal valorization of capital itself. The same motion that foresees the rise to prominence of a scientific discipline also announces its relegation. The fragmentation of the brain, the subdivision [*parcellarisation*] of intellectual tasks, calls out for a mediator, an image of the unified body. Nowadays we need more than the natural sciences; we need sciences of production, sciences of the brain, sciences of the relations between the disparate elements of the productive body. Psychology, sociology, linguistics, computer science are all disciplines that aspire to unity, all rivals in the race toward unity, already slaves of a dreamt-of unity that will subdivide [*parcellarisera*] each of them in turn. All of these sciences which have discovered in themselves the productive function that is bestowed upon them from the outside, and which have integrated it in their attempts to become themselves the sciences of mediation or communication, will be deceived. Their practitioners will rejoin the cohort of the dispossessed. History moves fast, the race for profit accelerates, and the internal crises of capitalism can't be exported the way they were in the early days of imperialism, because the cup is full and there's no more room. Nowadays crises are tossed from hand to hand the way you unload a firecracker that's about to explode. To call oneself to the attention of capitalism, to make vain boasts to the master about the value of the services one can provide, is already to dig one's own grave. No sooner appropriated than expropriated. Join the ranks of the dispossessed; no one has yet announced that intellectuals are finding their natural place at the side of proletarians who were dispossessed long before them. This concentration of malcontents at one pole of the social body, which supposedly isolates the great monopolies at the other, may be the sign of the revolt of the productive forces against overly constraining relations of production. But the proletarians are only concentrated as malcontents because their productivity has been dispossessed. Where has their productive force gone? And yet Marx was counting on them. In fact there are two ways of adopting the proletariat's perspective on the forces dominating history, two ways to "bank" on it. If critique is the point of view

94

of the future *as negation* of the present, Marx adopts the perspective of the proletariat insofar as he incarnates it. More generally, on history, it is necessary to adopt the perspective of non-history.

This perspective is not a chronological, phenomenological, or dialectical view from any identifiable future or conclusion of history, nor does its see the proletariat as a class that is historically produced by capitalism and destined to sublate it. The negation of history doesn't follow its affirmation, and doesn't overcome its negation. It needs to be understood as something that can never be deceived or dispossessed, that experiences [*connaît*] neither appropriation nor expropriation, nor property in any of its forms. The historical parade of structural opponents initially endowed by capital with productive properties, only to be expropriated for the profit of other producers (the peasantry, skilled artisans, worker proletariat, intellectual workers, every type of mediator), never attains the *radical* (i.e., beyond the categories of affirmation and negation) power of negation of the forces of non-history, which is always there, always untimely, and always resists the appropriating powers of the dialectic.

These structural and historical opponents are more like a paradoxical weed that springs furiously from the ground after every attack by an upside-down, appropriating-expropriating Attila, forcing him to attack again and again.

Part Two

Didier Deleule

Body-Machine and Living Machine

Husserl produces a myth and calls it Galileo. The myth is described as the "surreptitious substitution of idealized nature for prescientific sensible nature,"[24] and the results are well known. What Husserl refers to as the self-enclosed "garb of ideas" or "garb of symbols"[25] replaces the life-world with "'objectively actual and true' nature"[26] and everyone takes the forgery for the genuine article. This is simply the method employed by true being. The success of this disguise consists in the way it simultaneously discovers (it strips naked, it purifies) and conceals (it reveals prudishness about the body, which has to be dressed up in a garb of ideas). If the body is stripped bare in order to arrive at the purity of its mathematical essence, it also receives, at the same time, a new set of clothes that hide it from the indiscretion of immediate perception. The consequence of this disguising is that "the world of our sensible life is *merely* subjective" (emphasis added) and everything related to prescientific life is thereby "deprived of value".[27] The logical consequence is the abstraction of the subject's life as a person and of what Husserl calls "all cultural properties which are attached to things in human praxis."[28] This abstraction entails the split between the world of nature on the one hand and the world of spirit on the other, a split that Cartesianism thematizes in the project of a "naturalization of the psychic"[29] which will mark the modern era in its entirety. Merleau-Ponty further analyses the myth when he argues that psychologists missed the boat: the demotion of the body to the status of a random object, one object among others in a uniform, standardized world, blocks our perception of the body as a means of communication with the world even as it perverts the very notion of the world, which is now understood as a "collection of determinate objects," as opposed to "the latent horizon in all our experience"[30]

There seems to be, therefore, an original sin of psychology— confirmed by the emergence of scientific psychology in the nineteenth century—which establishes, in a single gesture, both a sharp limitation and a surprising extension of its object. The psychical object, reduced to a secondary reality that can be scientifically investigated, now finds itself, through the magic of this operation, vested with an objective reality that makes it a potential object of scientific understanding. It loses its singularity, but gains the dignity of participation in the universality of being. It finds its rightful place in the field of objective knowledge [savoir], even though this place deprives it of its unique, multi-faceted specificity. What is lost (for the knower [savant]) is of course subjective experience. What is now promoted is the identity of a being that can be represented and therefore mastered. Assessing the consequences of this prohibition on the value of bodily experience, Merleau-Ponty makes an accusation: "Psychologists did not realize that in treating the experience of the body in this way they were simply, in accordance with the scientific approach, shelving a problem which ultimately could not be avoided."[31] In fact, the ineptitude of the "psychologists" may not be the question at all; this shortcoming was swallowed up in the overall success of their discourse. What was also more or less unavoidable was their adventure in cosmetic surgery [chirurgie esthétique]: tidying up the body's proper meaning by scouring away all of its unmanageable and stubborn subjectivity, and replacing it with the marvelous intelligibility of finely-tuned gears, standardized and hence interchangeable. In short, they renewed the old Socratic injunction, but this time using industrial design [esthétique industrielle]. To put it another way: if psychologists missed the boat, this is not necessarily for reasons that belong essentially to psychology. It is more likely for reasons that the discipline of psychology participates in and relies on, but whose implications, as causes and effects, are never fully grasped. These are reasons that we will try to evoke briefly in the following pages, as we attempt to define a few milestones on the path that leads the productive body to construct psychology as an autonomous science.

Chapter I

The Construction of the Productive Body in its Own Image

I. The Cartesian Theory of the Body-Machine and of Life as Conquest

The Galilean "mythological" revolution, first of all, is not simply one aspect of a brutal subversion of medieval values.[32] Rather, it makes possible a simple image of the complex body, in which the denial of the validity of the vital forces in the epistemological field appears as the condition of possibility for the construction of the epistemological field itself. That is, the determination of the conditions of possibility for the production of a certain scientific knowledge [*savoir*], itself accredited as the condition of power [*pouvoir*] over things and over nature in general, reduced to a "mechanical toy."[33] The image of the body-machine is therefore drawn from both a definition of nature as an exuberant and omnipresent force [*puissance*], the sum of all possibles in which everyone may legitimately actualize themselves in determinate conditions that vary according to their virtue, and a redefinition of nature that excludes from its space a large set of possibles so as to allow only one to emerge at the expense of all others: nature as a uniform object suitable for mathematical treatment. This revolution is therefore less a subversion than a limitation, but the limitation is also a displacement. The boundless force [*puissance*] of irrational energies [*forces*] at work in the manifold of nature—against which only a carefully elaborated hierarchy of beings may sketch out an attempt at domination, i.e. may possibly prioritize the tasks to be accomplished and confer some dignity on their accomplishment—this boundless force is replaced by the idea of an eminent and unique dignity (eminent because outside the consideration of this privileged possible there is only waste and confusion; unique because nature is either one or it is nothing and the traditional bifurcation cannot determine pertinent rules allowing its explication) subject to invariable and uniform laws, rationally stipulated and therefore rationally discernable, if only by ordinary understanding armed with adequate methodological tools. What is radically new in the wake of this limitation/displacement is thus the idea that (scientific/technological) production is entirely *rational* in all its parts, i.e. explicable, justifiable, predictable and legitimate, stipulated and therefore efficient, recognizable and therefore manageable. This project of total rationality obviously had great implications for the representation of the body. The eviction of bodily experience from the epistemological field is accompanied by the promotion of an imaginary object (thematized in the theory of the body-machine), but also by the recognition of the body as the locus of vital experience (the realm of desire, of the power [*puissance*] of illusion and deceit, but at the same time of the necessity for guidance in life).[34] To conclude that the real of experience is therefore outfoxed by the imaginary of representation would be to miss the point of the "First Meditation" entirely. On the other hand, what is set in motion here is a certain type of separation. What is separated analytically is not soul from body, the sovereign soul faced with a subjugated body; on the contrary, it is the de facto union of the soul and the body in what Descartes calls the "composite," which, as a first, albeit problematic phenomenon, makes possible the potential separation-abstraction of the body conceived as a pure machine submitted to the ordinary laws of mechanics. In fact, therefore, the body is always unified with the soul; but this factual, empirical, determinate union does not fail to raise the question of the ambiguous status of the very notion of the body.[35] Thus it is only from a juridical perspective that we can separate the body as a pure machine and treat it in an autonomous manner. This juridical separation is what Cartesianism accounts for.

We need to be precise. It's not life that imitates the machine; life is not reduced to the mechanical. It is the machine itself that simulates life.[36] This is the crucial point that authorizes the seemingly incomprehensible, even scandalous displacement that takes place, these days, on the level of language, in the affirmation, for example, that there should be an *adaptation* of machine to man. The apparent representational perversion that understands living beings through the model of the machine appears as one of the conditions of possibility for the reinforced exploitation of the body-machine, but this perversion is only a perversion for the humanist gesture that points it out in order to denounce it. This representational perversion actually draws its meaning from a more profound, and profoundly violent gesture that gives the image of a living thing a mechanical structure because the body—become an imaginary object—now projects its vital energy into a self-enclosed mechanism which in principle holds no surprises, and because this projection is only sustainable insofar as it ultimately refers back to the organism as the object which is imitated in the ends of a now-enlarged productivity. For what this metamorphosis brings about is first and foremost an increase in power [*pouvoir*]. Without an understanding of this fundamental point, the entire process may remain mysterious. In effect, the idea is not that the machine should be able to replace living things in a project of conquest that is impossible for them, but rather that in its essence life is conquest and that the machine, to accomplish its function, must be inscribed in a motion that prolongs that of the living organism.[37] That this simulation remains a simulation, i.e. an approximation and never a fusion, changes nothing. The body-machine is both life affirmed in all the exuberance of its dominating movement, and the machine required for the development of effective potentialities, required as the guarantee of functional movement.[38] Thus we are not in the presence of a simple descriptive tool. This is not simply a manner of speaking, nor is it a simplification for pedagogical purposes. To the contrary, it is, in a certain way, the affirmation of the powers [*puissances*] of the vital energy that confronts "nature" as a privileged point of application, an object of mastery and conquest which is itself machine-like. At the same time, this also provides the means for undertaking the infinite task of conquest; the body-machine is the machine that always takes something from life, more or less skillfully simulating it, but that always remains indebted to it for its very conception. The theory of the body-machine therefore appears, in the same motion, as both the discovery and the covering-up of the very essence of technology. To fulfill this "machination," life had to be reduced to the machine in accordance with the very image of life, and the machine had to be given for what it is, namely, the extension (even if by inanimate forces) of life, i.e., that which inscribes itself in the same trajectory as life and not that which substitutes for it.[39] Consequently, the machine does not replace life and was never supposed to. All the fine argumentation about how a wrongly organized "society" increases work even though the means of production could provide relief for the worker-citizen via a potential politics of leisure activities, and similarly certain directions in cybernetics research, fail to recognize this fundamental characteristic of Western civilization: the machine is not constructed to replace life in its servile tasks. In no way does it replace life's function of mastery and conquest; rather, its function is to augment the power [*pouvoir*] of life itself understood as the development of the process of mastery over nature. Indeed, it is precisely on the basis of this image of a conquering, expansionist, and imperialist life, of life in a stance of aggression towards nature, that the epistemological myth of a body-machine takes shape and that the discourse of the mechanic, engineer, and inventor is freed to develop. If simulation remains essentially mechanical, some thinkers, with the help of electronic tortoises or other animal devices,[40] still hold out hopes of unlocking the secret of "adaptation" as the principle characteristic behind the behavior of living beings.[41] The adaptation of the machine to man therefore can only signify, at bottom, the mechanical simulation of the very project of life, and the body-machine must therefore be understood as the epistemological paradigm built from this same project.

Why is it, then, that humanist protests see the paradigm as a representational perversion? What Engels refers to as "the victory of machine-work over hand-work"[42] makes the identification of manual and machine work necessary. This is the historical *feedback* [in English in the original] that results from the progressive destruction of the independent producer, from his progressive proletarization, the con game [*marché de dupes*] that reveals the apparent representational perversion as the sign of a real expropriation, and that, without effacing the imprint of the living model, makes economy responsible for overturning an image that is lived as such by workers. The revolt of living work against its replacement by dead work, life's refusal to submit to death, **still points toward** an obscure feeling that the two projects are somehow the same. The machine competes with workers just as workers compete with one another in the labor market (where their loss of independence inaugurates the era of "liberty"), and the first process exacerbates the second, eventually drawing women and children into the system of generalized competition.[43] But at the same time, the mechanical work of living beings subjugated to the machine is experienced by them as a reduction to the simulation of a deathly activity, as a theft of life, as an extortion of vital energy by the rhythmic task that enforces identification with the machine. This is the contradiction: on the one hand the obscure recognition that the machine is part of a certain vital "project" (tragically indicating the generalized competition inside the productive body), and on the other the notion that the biological body is a tool reduced to a machinified process (which may in fact be the case, but only through the magic of a reversal of the image). Throughout the history of the worker's movement, revolutionary strategies and tactics have reflected one or the other side of this contradiction, and sometimes both.

To insist on the machinified perception of the biological body is therefore to refer to a representation of living beings in which work's production is constitutive of the perceived being: the pure work machine, with its blemishes of subjectivity scoured away, with its idleness and laziness denounced and condemned as the incarnation of social evil. The body-machine appears in its historical destiny as productive being, not because the machine's encounter with the body might be productive, but because life itself, in its project of conquest, must be presented as productive power [*puissance*]. Because the machine is an extension of life's activity, the very representation of the body-machine gives life its essence as part of a "conspiracy" that was spun elsewhere. If the living being must become machine, this is because the machine accumulates the potentialities that were inscribed in the living being even as it seems to allow it to save its vital energy. In fact, isn't it this appearance of energy-saving that encourages the myth that there is a replacement or "liberation" of energies [*forces*] for other non-productive tasks, the illusion of the body's free energy [*énergie*], even though rest is only recuperation; drink and drugs [*"l'assomoir"*] only a supplementary marking of the body; and intensive sports, a recently promoted antidote to work, simply another form of ascetics, a strenuous discipline of self-mutilation? What is implied in the representation of the body-machine is therefore the progressive reduction of the manual act to a mechanical operation, even before the machine purely and simply replaces the mechanical gesture. But it consequently appears that this gesture itself is both the reduction of the skilled, complex task to its simplest expression, and the simulation of living work.[44] The result is that this implication will only be justified in its historical "effects" which will uphold the representation, without the invocation of any theory of "reflection."

2. The Theory of the Body-Machine as a Tool for Conceptualizing the Construction of the Productive Body

The theory of the body-machine implies something different than the apparent reduction of the living being to a machine. This is part of it, certainly, but it also reveals a clever move that allows the production of such an image. In fact, both movements are inseparable and this is what gives them their exemplary quality. The availability of the body's organs for various movements makes it possible to dispense with the soul as productive principle. Thus the automaton is a "work of nature" too.[45] In such a way that death becomes contemporaneous with the rupture brought about by mechanical organization, that the soul cannot take responsibility for it, and that the disappearance of the substantial relation is only a consequent manifestation of its mechanical cancellation. But that the machine's destruction can lead to such consequences for the living-human means that we must think of the end intrinsic to the organization of cogs making up the machine as the revelation of a plan that is outside the functioning of the machine itself.[46] Here the Cartesian analysis goes considerably beyond its immediate concerns. What it helps us think through is the ruse by which the productive body constructs itself. In retracing this path, we will therefore not be adopting Borkenau's thesis about a mechanical era understood as the ideological reflection of the organizational mode of manufacture.[47] Much more profoundly, (Cartesian) mechanism's theory of the body-machine brings to light the process, inherent to technology, which consists in withdrawing natural and immediate finality from living beings in order to transfer it in a mediated and secret manner to a domain that remains foreign to the living being.

We can conceptualize the construction of the productive body thanks to the juridical separation of the body-machine. The real increase in power [*pouvoir*] seized in this manner accompanies the radical reorientation of the supposed relations of the living organism with nature. And this reorientation also necessitates an intelligible homogeneity of acting forces. Thus it is not *only* in order to make itself better known, or to be better disciplined, no doubt, that the body undergoes this mechanical treatment. What is at stake is a certain power [*puissance*]: the body-machine's power pushes back against the power of mechanical nature. The homogenizing effect of this treatment corresponds not to some cosmological fusion, but to the emergence of a situation that must be perceived as antagonistic. The body-machine and the world-machine confront one another, each using the same mechanisms. Yet homogeneity does not imply balance: what exceeds the project of conquest introduces a certain imbalance of the forces that constitute humanity's part in life. If the completed paradigm of the body-machine, or the animal-machine, is the *telos* of intelligibility for man-machine, it also undergoes a real deprivation, for it becomes that which lacks reason, i.e. language, calculation, the projection of ends.[48]

Thus, beyond the project of total intelligibility of which it is a part, the theory of the body-machine appears as the recognition and exploitation of a new characteristic of life: life as conquest and domination of nature. And simultaneously, the body-machine incarnates the ruse in which a transfer of finality expels living beings from the project altogether. What emerges is the possibility of conceptualizing the productive body as the consequence of the breakdown of relations between man and nature; humanity smashing its way through nature, following a plan it can never quite figure out.

In order for the productive body to construct itself, the fragmentation of the biological body must have taken place in such a way that its lost unity can only be recovered through an epistemic apprehension that does not exclude the specialization of tasks. The productive act must be withdrawn from the body itself, from living work, so that it can take refuge in the specialized gesture that draws its significance and effectiveness entirely from its status as the organ of a unique function that guarantees its infallibility, but which is included in a general mechanism whose meaning cannot be grasped by the actor and which, in its very development, marks the actor's body in a way that transforms him, as in the fable of Menenius Agrippa, into a metonymic representation of himself in which one fragment of the body becomes the body as a whole.

Now, to move things toward their conclusions, let us see how this representation becomes more refined, and how it becomes enriched with new determinations, so to speak, to the point that it necessitates, for the examination of its particularity, the constitution of a specific discipline, a scientific psychology, at the heart of the fully-developed productive body. This transition, which implies the recognition of a new concept of life, will also be the transition from the "co-operation" of tasks specialized and defined under a central control to the vast self-regulating automaton, pure image of the productive body, now obligated to maintain the illusion of a co-operation that is lost but still wished-for.

Chapter II

Psychology within the Productive Body

I. Psychology as "Organology"; or, the Living Machine and its Contradictions

Whether we find it reassuring or frightening, everyone is impressed by the spectacle of scientific scrutiny zeroing in on carefully chosen specimens of productivity. The sense of touch is naturally our first object of analysis: since it provides access to exteriority and functions as our primary organ of manipulation, it has legitimate claims to precedence as an object of systematic enquiry, claims that are well established in the philosophical tradition. But what do we touch, and who does the touching? Bodies, no doubt, but bodies that resist, bodies that are heavy, that push, that may be hot or cold,[49] and above all bodies that never get tired of deceiving the senses about their own judgments, bodies that delude us because a sense excited in this manner by exteriority is prone to illusions about itself and unreliability toward its object. This means that a much more thorough exploration needs to be organized. We'll need to examine the entire surface of the body spread out in space like the hide of a skinned animal stretched flat. We'll need an instrument to measure tactile sensitivity: a pair of iron calipers, with cork tips on the ends. We'll use our instrument to systematically examine the entire surface of the skin and adjoining mucosal tissues (the tongue, lips, etc.). This will reveal that maximum sensitivity, capable of distinguishing minimal pressure in two adjacent spots, is located at the tip of the tongue and on the inside surface of the fingertips; that this sensitivity diminishes as we proceed from the extremity of each limb toward the trunk; and that the back has very poor sensory receptivity. We will note that sensitivity to the tips of the calipers is greater if they make contact with the epidermis one after another and not simultaneously. We will also learn that when the subject moves the finger in contact with the esthesiometer, he senses the double contact more rapidly; and thus, generally, that moving the organs of touch greatly increases their sensitivity. And, finally, we will learn that, in order for the subject to perceive the double contact, the tips of the calipers must separated by a minimum of 1 millimeter on the tip of the tongue; 2 millimeters on the inside surface of the fingertips. All these findings rest on the hypothesis that (tactile) sensitivity is identical in all individuals and that different organisms all obey laws of homogeneity similar to those that apply to machines. But at the same time we must admit that, although this machine cannot "objectively" err, its understanding of its own functioning may remain "subjectively" problematic. This is evident in the instructions for an experiment on the sensation of touch: "Be alert; we will periodically touch the back of your hand very lightly. It is easy to be mistaken, so be careful in answering 'yes' each time you think you feel contact. If you're unsure, just rely on your first impressions."[50] During the experiment itself, we need to be alert for "errors of suggestibility or fraud" and use a thousand little tricks, for example by asking the question when there has been no contact. Our development of "objective" techniques must therefore maintain constant suspicion toward the discourse it evaluates. Here language is not only what hollows out the gulf between man and machine; as something necessary yet superfluous, as a simple signal of sensation, language also constitutes the medium in which the machine is called upon to deceive itself about its own relation to the world. Or even worse, to lie for reasons it can't even comprehend. The problem for the mechanistic universe is always the same: where does the error come from? What is the cause of the deception, the negative?

Modern psychology constitutes itself as an attempt to minimize this embarrassing "subjectivity." No matter what, the lips will always be the part of the body most sensitive to touch, followed by the skin that covers the tips of the fingers and toes. No matter what, a given weight will feel heavier if we lift it with our left hand. No matter what, the perceived difference between an ounce and a dram (cf. Weber, "Prolegomena XII") will remain the same even when standards of comparison change in quantity and absolute intensity. In other words, the subject has no right to be mistaken. His error may be a fact, but he has no right to it. And as for lies (whether motivated by gullibility, laziness, irony, irritation, or sheer malice), these can be countered by a higher trickery, a new version of the old adage that all men are either fools or knaves.

In its early stages, the goal and accomplishment of the discipline and its "applications" is to foresee the useless or mistaken gesture, to adapt the living machine to the dead one, to make the living machine function like a dead machine — without problems, without qualms, and above all without wasting time — to transform the living machine entirely into efficacious motion. This is before the appearance of those problems of "relation" in which affectivity makes its triumphal return and grafts itself onto the main body of the discipline. We examine sensitivity to pressure, temperature, pain, and electricity; to burning, brushing, twisting, tickling sensations; and to subcutaneous, vibrating, or kinetic sensations. No stone is left unturned and no hiding-place for hints of subjectivity left unexamined as the exploration extends across the entire bodily surface. And as we know so well, exploration can, in certain circumstances, lead to colonization.

The eye is our next object. The eye as precious auxiliary of the hand, guiding the hand in its efficacy with geometric precision, yet ultimately subject to error, as we know, for example, from the persistence of observational error even in the Transit Room of the Greenwich Observatory. Yet this apparent error can be accounted for by the fallibility of the individual. Accurate measurements of vision and visual accuracy will have to take account of "reaction time," understood as the delay between the production of an external stimulus (whether visual, audible, olfactory, gustatory, and so on) and the external motion by which the subject indicates his perception of the sensation provoked by the stimulus.[51] The importance accorded to reaction time bears witness to the effort exerted to eliminate the influence of subjectivity as far as possible in order to refine the precision of measurement. The duration of modifications to consciousness takes priority over their intensity, for example in the work of Wilhelm Wundt and his school. In this manner the living machine, in cases of simple or complex reaction, undergoes a new reduction, for this manner of conceptualizing the system signifies one thing only: the intensity of the productive gesture depends on the duration of the reaction to stimulus, and not the reverse. But reciprocally, the duration of the reaction time depends on the intensity of the stimulation of the sensory organs. The more intense the stimulation, the quicker the reaction. On average, light stimuli produce slower reactions, whereas sound and touch tend to produce faster reactions. Thus an intensive increase in stimulation, by shortening the duration of reaction time, can lead to an acceleration of the pace of production. Everything is a question of rhythm, but getting into rhythm can be life-threatening if the machine breaks down as it tries to improve. The machine produces more, but, as everyone observes, the results are less satisfactory; who cares about quality when quantity alone is required? Nevertheless, the instrument remains precious; when the production of absolute surplus-value (lengthening the work day) reaches its limits, emphasis shifts to the production of relative surplus-value (acceleration of the pace of work). In *Capital*, volume I, chapter 16, Marx demonstrates that while the production of absolute surplus-value depends solely on the duration of work, the production of relative surplus-value "completely revolutionizes the technical processes of labor and the groupings into which society is divided." "It therefore requires," he concludes, "a specifically capitalist mode of production" [645]. But the program still requires implementation. The system needs perfecting and, from its emergence in the middle of the nineteenth century, modern psychology envisions a future that it has been consolidating ever since. Make no mistake: psychology is neither a simple ideological reflection of a capitalist mode of production, nor its transparent effect. It patiently follows the twists and turns of a grand historical project animated by a dead subject. It accompanies it, upholds it, distinguishes itself from it, and returns to it. It is always *there*, a seemingly indispensable gear in the social machinery, always performing its intervention quietly but all the more effectively.

In studying "two-sided phenomena," in Ribot's terminology, the psychologist develops rigorous research techniques in order to determine the specificity of the psychical apparatus. But these techniques are also motivated by the need to account for errors and sensory illusion, and to refer their causes not to immediate subjectivity, but rather to the intellectual processes that ordinarily accompany it. The principle of parallelism,[52] whatever its modalities (consciousness attributed to all vital phenomena; consciousness reduced to more or less independent physiological syntheses; consciousness limited to a minimal zone of physiological acts), always affirms the automatism of the body and refuses, in any circumstance, to grant consciousness the character of an active force (whatever other attributes one may allow it). Consciousness can only be epiphenomenal.[53] Thus the polemical implication of parallelism, as a scientific postulate, consists in dispensing with the "metaphysical" hypothesis—now considered useless and costly, i.e. ruinous—of any sort of interaction between the body and consciousness. If physical and mental phenomena become merely concurrent and any immediate causality of the body on the mind disappears, this implies a scale of beings in which the hypothesis of vital phenomena with no need of consciousness nevertheless can never entail the possibility of consciousness and its acts apart from the presence of the body. The bodily machine functions without receiving its orders from consciousness; yet, always present at the highest level of the hierarchy of beings, consciousness accompanies it without acting. Thus the machine moves by itself and the soul is reduced to a lesser function as the "logical subject of internal experience."[54] It's not surprising, then, that the precise formulation of the problem becomes that of the relations between the soul and the body:

> Psychophysics should be understood here as an exact theory of the functionally dependent relations of body and soul, or, more generally, of the material and the mental, of the physical and the psychological worlds.... All discussions and investigations of psychophysics relate only to the apparent phenomena of the material and mental worlds, to a world that either appears directly through introspection or through outside observation, or that can be deduced from its appearance or grasped as a phenomenological relationship.... Briefly, psychophysics refers to the *physical* in the sense of physics and chemistry, to the *psychical* in the sense of experimental psychology, without referring back in any way to the nature of the body or of the soul beyond the phenomenal in the metaphysical sense.[55]

But in the end, the transition from substance to phenomenon cannot mask the difficulty psychology experiences as it attempts to define the status of the psychical "side" of things. This is why, for example, researchers like Exner attempt to determine the duration of the properly psychological phases of reaction time in order to measure the duration of supposedly elementary intellectual operations.[56] These efforts produce experiments whose principles are simple but whose outcomes remain enigmatic.

Once we arrive at a precise calculation of the duration of the would-be non-psychological phases, the total obtained in this manner is subtracted from the overall duration of reaction time. The specific duration of the conscious phase is thus expressed in this simple difference. So in other words, what is conscious is the result of a subtraction: what does not evidently belong to the machine-automaton in its perceived functioning may be attributed, without too much confusion, to the action of consciousness. No psychologist, in any event, ever disputes the difficulty of the undertaking. Another experiment utilizes a black box or camera obscura 25 centimeters long, with a blank sheet of paper (9x11 centimeters) at one end. At the other end, the subject's eye looks at the paper from a 3-centimeter circular hole. A Geissler tube [early form of neon tube] lights up the box whenever current flows through it. In the main circuit, the needle of a chronoscope moves whenever the current in the secondary circuit lights up the box and the white paper. When the timing mechanism is started, the noise from the chronoscope indicates to the subject that the experiment has begun. The operation proceeds:

1. The subject closes the secondary circuit half way; the observer starts the chronoscope, but the needles don't move because the current is still in the main circuit.
2. The observer completely closes the secondary circuit and the light goes on; as the main circuit is weakened the needles start moving.
3. As soon as the subject perceives the light on the white paper, he raises his hand and interrupts the secondary circuit; the light goes off and the current returns to the main circuit, stopping the needles immediately.

The result obtained is a precise measurement, to the thousandth of a second, of the time that has passed between the moment the subject "saw" the light on the white surface and the moment he signaled his perception by moving his hand. The visual or color stimuli could of course be varied ad infinitum. But the rest is only a matter of subtraction. So where's the rub? In two places, it appears, even if we accept the technical precision of the experiment. First, there is individual variation in the physical reaction of raising one's arm. Thus general psychology can't do without individual psychology, or a psychology of differences as well as a psychology of similarities. Behind the beautiful homogeneity of the machine lies the threatening heterogeneity of subjects. Second, who can guarantee that the subject with the raised arm is indeed reacting at the moment when he is supposed to react. Whether a delay is voluntary or involuntary, the period of the duration of consciousness unexpectedly increases. And what about the duration of complex conscious phenomena (choices, associations, judgments, etc.)? The psychologist arrives at a cautious conclusion: "the psychophysiological work undertaken to date to measure the duration of conscious phenomena provides indications rather than results."[57] This caution is entirely legitimate and points toward the true status of psychology. All of the research that attempts to develop the concept of a psycho-physical divide, or to determine what would constitute a "free" act or "pure" thought outside corporeal conditioning, only leads us back to a reconsideration of the system as a whole. What is a "free" act, if not a "readaptation"? Now the substantialist soul-body dualism is replaced by an organism-milieu dualism (and the Darwinian model steps into a supporting role). The object of psychology is not consciousness, but the individual subject negotiating its surrounding milieu. Psychology will be initially conceptualized as one part of biology, and its essential problem, not yet formulated as such, will be the survival of the individual in its social milieu: "In relation to their environment, all organisms are in a state of equilibrium that fluctuates around a theoretical point of perfect adaptation."[58] This is therefore the task of modern psychology: to proceed in such a manner that the living machine, in its ordinary functioning, becomes as adapted as possible to the social mechanism into which it is, in fact, integrated, so that that its productive act develops in optimal conditions and its gears don't grind too loudly. The fact of consciousness has no real specificity; outside the doubleness or doubling of the science, it slips from our grasp. The only legitimate object of scientific investigation is the corporeal machine, the organ of transmission and adaptive energy. The concurrence of consciousness and corporeal machine is noted, and this renders the status of the former element permanently enigmatic, transforming all scientific desire about it into fiction: "The goal of parallelism is precisely this: to put what is called the mind, this imaginary edifice constructed through the centuries, back into its real home, the body, and to locate within it the body's higher functions."[59] The goal of our work will be precisely to determine what sort of body this is, how it is put together, and how it sustains itself.

Psychology aims to be a "psychology without a soul."[60] This means first that it renounces metaphysics and refuses even to take a position on the existence of its substance. At this point the concurrent psychical element is perceptible only in the subject's essential capacity to exert and control its attention. J.-F. Richard has very clearly shown how the discovery of the fact of individual differences was a tremendous obstacle for the first attempts at psychological measurement.[61] Attempts to determine a personal equation, part of reaction time research, lead to the idea of variations in attention, but at the same time, necessitate a displacement that refers variations between individuals back to variations within the individual. Consequently, "what is studied is not reaction time, but reaction time insofar as it translates the duration of the process of apperception" [Richard]. The result is the measurement of the duration of the process. Of its nature, however, nothing can be said. Here, obviously, the rights of the concurrent psychical element reassert themselves. While the intensity of the productive gesture depends on the duration of the stimulated reaction time, attention still has to be controlled by the observer, and still has to be exercised by the subject itself. The duration we measure is only a sign of the living machine's aptitude for increasing its output. And of course the organ has its limits. Bouguer demonstrated this with his experiment that determined the brightness at which one light prevents the eye from perceiving another light of lesser brightness. The disappearance of one candle's shadow on a white screen illuminated by another candle requires 7 feet of separation between the two: "the distance between the two lights remained visible until the more distant source was approximately 64 times weaker than the main source."[62] But these sorts of problems, affecting astronomers and physicists, are not only opportunities to steal away even more of the psychical element's potential function; they also fit into a conception of the living machine that the pioneering psychologist will develop in his particular manner. What interests the psychologist is less the intrinsic limits of the senses, but the play of reactions that lead the machine into errors as it judges distance, size, sound, and touch. The machine itself cannot be at fault; it does what it is supposed to do. So responsibility for the errors falls upon the concurrent psychical element. Illusions and errors stem less from the machine itself than from the failure—perhaps basic, but correctible nevertheless—of its controlling instruments. The higher the level of intellectuality, the higher the risk of error: "certain intellectual operations superimpose themselves onto the simpler operations of elementary sensory judgments, providing perceptions that often mislead the subject as to the nature of the perceived phenomena, as happens in most optical illusions."[63] For example: In comparing two weights with different volumes, if a visual perception of the two volumes precedes the comparison, then the weight of the smallest volume will always be overestimated. This is the familiar contrast of the kilo of feathers and the kilo of lead: "sight only degrades the muscles' ability to discern weight."[64] Apparently the only subjects who escape the illusion are the feeble-minded, which provides a sort of experimental confirmation. The more of an idiot one is, the less one reflects (the more one is short-sighted, in the metaphorical sense of the expression); and the less one reflects, the quicker and more precise the action. The senses do not mislead us. Kant and the others were right: it is the understanding that wreaks havoc with the machine's wonderful ordinance. It is the eye, the "noblest" sense organ, the paradigm of intellect, which correlates most closely with the concurrent psychical element. The eye is the organ of ambivalence: in it is concentrated the psychical manifestation of reaction (I see and raise my arm; I see and press the button); in it we locate the specificity of the psychical approached in this manner, its attention and duration. Thus the eye produces by means of vicarious gestures.[65] But the eye also leads to errors in judgment and obstructs the efficacious gesture. Who can undertake to rectify these errors? Who can repair the perfect productive circuit potentially disrupted by the inevitable yet distracting concurrent psychical element? As Diderot puts it, "we are blind, and the eye is the dog that leads us." And he promptly adds, "how misleading this organ (the eye) would be, if its judgments were not constantly rectified by the sense of touch."[66] His words could easily be those of modern psychology at its beginnings. For in the end, the only ideal machine would be a blind one; not an oedipal machine putting out its eyes to achieve vision, but rather a machine born to blindness, and thus furnished with a world which is different yet complete, in which every problem can be resolved through touch, in which robotic hands become part of the wonderful mechanical repetition of the productive gesture. No more need to be concerned with adaptation, and he'd better not ask about having those cataracts removed! That's how we put an end to the story of the eye. Without sight, illusion is minimized. Life just complicates things: the eye sparkles, the eye seduces, it's the window of the soul. This is not about the blank eyes of ancient statues, but rather the absence of the eye: this will be the *telos* of the living machine. Without the deceitful sight of its hidden dwarf, Maelzel's chess-playing automaton—perceived in its immediateness—would be rigorous perfection. But sight is the possibility of inattention, of the simple distraction that compounds the very fact of the error even as it lays bare the dupe's illusion. Whatever else we can say about it, the machine is not concerned with problems of adaptation: the way it functions is necessarily adequate to its function. Only life poses these questions, and sight mirrors it in this respect; thus the notion of accommodation[67] belongs to optics as much as to biology. Functionalism was intended to take responsibility for this kind of representation. We refer not only to its combined critique of "structuralism" and the psychology of the faculties, or the way it substitutes the individual's adjusting and adapting coordination for the constellation of elements that make up unique acts of living beings in constant interaction with the environment;[68] we speak more particularly of its instrumental theory of the mind that gives rise to contemporary operationalism. The important thing in this theory is that mental activity is reduced to an organ that can be transformed through experience, and that can be perfected (this is how psychology codifies the concept of conditioning). The mind, with all its active or inactive attributes of attention, surveillance, control, decision, etc., is therefore not a guide, properly speaking, but rather a pure instrument utilized by the living machine for its unique adaptive end, just as it uses sensory organs. No qualitative distinction can be allowed, therefore, between mental activity and nervous activity; mind represents what is simply a quantitatively higher stage of the living machine's adjustment process.[69] The concurrent psychical element gives no commands. As only one aspect of the living machine, it takes its orders from a selection process that calls on it to perform effective techniques for ensuring survival. In other words, simply living is no longer sufficient; now it's necessary to learn how to survive.

James McKeen Cattell, pioneering the notion of the "mental test," developed a series of categories for measuring this process: "I) Dynamometer Pressure; II) Rate of Movement; III) Sensation-areas; IV) Pressure causing Pain; V) Least Noticeable difference in Weight; VI) Reaction-time for Sound; VII) Time for naming Colors; VIII) Bi-section of a 50 cm. Line; IX) Judgment of 10 seconds time; X) Number of Letters remembered on once Hearing."[70]

Cattell's entire argument consists in showing that this type of research, although it might seem to imply a physiological perspective, was of great interest to the psychologist because it is "impossible to separate bodily from mental energy." What is measured by dynamometer pressure, for example, is the "'sense of effort'" and the "effects of volition on the body." Obtaining "the greatest possible squeeze of the hand" sets in motion a whole series of hitherto unsuspected relations between "volitional control" and "bodily power" or between "emotional excitement" and that same bodily power [374].[71] Moreover, it would be a mistake to underestimate the psychological bearings of the connections between rate of movement and force of movement: how can we figure out a way to keep the rate of movement from decreasing the precision and force of movement? It's a question of "temperaments," no doubt, even though repeated measurements with the chronoscope open up the possibility of improving performance, albeit only after adaptive conditioning that confirms the importance of selecting the best subjects. Temporal and spatial judgment becomes crucial for gauging the precision of the efficacious gesture: "divide an ebony rule (3 cm. wide) into two equal parts by means of a movable line"; "strike on the table with the end of a pencil and again after 10 seconds, and let the experimentee in turn strike when he judges an equal interval to have elapsed." For both tests, "allow only one trial" [377]. In short: estimate reaction time.

So it is not enough to merely say, here, that the body is being conceived as a machine, or even as a machine whose maintenance requires the evaluation of its potential and the regulation of its functioning. Nothing in that description distinguishes this representation from that of classical mechanics. What these lists reveal, in fact—through the pertinent techniques—is essentially a process whereby the living machine is integrated into the general system of the fully developed productive body.[72] The biological body—understood as an ensemble of organs directly or indirectly plugged into the exterior world—now takes its place in a mechanism with finely tuned and hopefully well-oiled cogs, inside the great productive body, where its function as a necessary part recalls its primordial productive function. In other words, the biological body itself becomes the servant of the productive body (and this image immediately replaces any other possible image). Henceforth the biological body must be perceived as both a basic element or constitutive part and as the overall system of the developed productive body. If the biological body can serve the machine, this is because it is already machine-like in its ordinary functioning; and the disappearance of its desire signals an implicit acknowledgement that the desired isomorphism will not be troubled by any symbolic debts. In this manner the Leviathan's dream is fulfilled: absorbed by the social body, the biological body is forced to accept identification with a narrow representation based on its supposedly natural limits and richly compensated efforts. Since the machine does not think, it can be programmed, and it always requires stimulation. It's a strange machine which is contradictory in its very being; while not haunted by cogitation, it can't seem to avoid the *ratiocinatio*. This brings us to the eruption of a new dimension of desire—to be called "motivation"—which will culminate in the kind of full-blown Taylorism that is still much-debated by labor "managers" [*"responsables"*] today.[73]

2. Survival as the Real Theme of Modern Psychology

Thus we arrive at one of the fundamental teachings of modern psychology, namely, that we survive only by submitting to the demands of death. The dominant theme of adaptation points toward the necessity of integrating the living machine into the "mechanics of death." Survival, in a certain way, means becoming a servant of death, i.e., accepting that the very conditions of life are controlled, so to speak, by an outside organism following a plan whose complexities may provide an illusion of autonomy but ultimately reveal themselves as elements of an alien body. It is undoubtedly at this level that we see most clearly the implications of the early influence of biological models on psychology: the condition of possibility of the individual subject's survival in the social milieu is the subject's submission to the demands of selection, itself a product of the law of competition. Or as Gladstone put it, "human life is but, in nine cases out of ten, a struggle for existence."[74] In this manner adaptation, as a dynamic process and operational necessity of life itself, comes to be understood as a necessary but not entirely sufficient condition of survival. The recurrent theme of survival, circulating in a thousand bitterly ironic slogans and clichés, is far from naïve; it acknowledges the underlying ambiguity of the notion of survival. For there to be survival, there must be victory in struggle. Therefore it must be surrounded by death. But the survivor, marked from the very beginning by the death which produces him, is himself only a trial run for death and thus the opposite of life. The survivor exemplifies the basic biological subsistence, the well-paced rhythm which, in its very repetition, reveals itself as the loss of energy; and he performs the adaptive gesture that introduces the paradigm of submission to the forces of death. Not as the emergence of some sort of foreordained technological destiny, of course, but as the tightly woven network created by the system that absorbs living work. In a singular movement, the adaptive process incessantly demanded by the system of the productive body therefore affirms the virtues of consumption as a condition of the individual's "biological" survival, while also emphasizing the importance of conditioning processes and the necessary development of new abilities as the mechanisms on which the subject's "social" survival is predicated. Whether one of these processes can take precedence over the other is a delicate question, even though liberal discourses tend to insist on the development of the former while technocratic discourses are inclined to promote the latter. For behind the façade, it is really a single process with mutually reinforcing elements, in which gains concerning "biological" survival (i.e. the minimum rate of consumption required to maintain the system) can be referred to as "abundance," while "social" survival, now reduced to purely technological criteria, appears as the possibility of "promotion."

But while, for the time being, the historical destiny of the living machine appears to point toward a progressive downsizing of the living element and a conclusive preponderance of the machine element, the development of modern psychology intervenes in this process somewhat discordantly. The discipline's entire evolution and very existence seems to indicate the impossibility of a total mechanization of life. Psychology—and this is why we arrive at a concern with adaptation—is thus the necessary acknowledgement of the irreducible presence of life in the living machine. At its beginnings, modern psychology constitutes the highest effort to scientifically characterize living beings as machines, i.e., as cogs in the productive body. But this effort also marks the failure of attempts to remove life from the body-machine system. What is affirmed in this manner is the potential of a two-fold definition of life as conquest and as survival. Within the identity implied by this principle, the vital project of conquest clashes with a homogeneous alterity as it attempts to realize itself, and this clash transforms the goal of co-operation into a perpetual threat, a battlefield separating the realms of life and death. If the emergence of scientific psychology marks the failure of the mechanization of life, despite the demands that constitute its primary allegiance, this is because its role is to proffer a particular resolution of the problem of survival, to turn back the course of this imaginary history and reaffirm the goal of co-operation, or in other words to determine optimal conditions for adaptation, to foresee all risks of conflict,[75] to substitute the peace of machines for the war of living beings, and to reinforce the notion that the productive body is homogeneous and that its members and organs divide and share their functions according to an unchangeable plan.

The biological body is a cog in the productive body, yet remains separate from it. And this separation is certainly not the beneficial result of a logical abstraction that would promote the organic machine while distinguishing from it the exuberance of bodily experience. The separation that takes place here is part of the larger representation of a relatively autonomous, self-sustaining ensemble whose force is applied through the workmanlike automaton. That the body appears as a cog is thus not incompatible with its apparent autonomy. In fact it requires it, just as the market requires the individual's "freedom" to sell his labor-power [*force de travail*]. Dependent and dominated (separated from the means of production), the body is never-theless perceived as autonomous; it functions freely in the same sense that the parts of a machine function smoothly once the machine is set in motion. Whereas the functioning of a machine is *obviously* dependent, the biological body is enveloped by a complex representation in which mechanical functioning is everywhere haunted by life. And consequently the productive body poses the apparently contradictory problems of the necessity of increasing productivity and of the individual's survival within a system of vital competition. On the one hand, the mechanical representation of the biological body invariably reduces it to the status of a cog; but on the other hand it remains true that the biological body is biological before it becomes mechanical. The life that once appeared conquering now appears increasingly threatened, and demands new ways of posing the unavoidable question, that of survival.

If the producer is separated from the means of production, this is not the outcome of some abstraction, but the result of a real historical process, the history of an expropriation. And it seems that this fundamental separation can only occur as the result of a progressive synthesis taking place in the general mechanism itself, where the juxtaposition of all of the system's elements—the condition of the system's proper functioning—requires the auto-functioning of the biological body as the most basic element of the pyramid, as the condition of possibility for the permanence of the system itself. If the organism must be a machine, this machine itself must be organic in its ordinary functioning. If life is reintroduced into the mechanical universe in this manner, this is because it is necessary to the composition of a beautiful functional totality grounded in the body's sensorial and intellectual potentialities. Each organ fulfills a multiplicity of functions, but initially only the relation to exteriority is taken into account. Thus the organism-environment dualism schematized in the stimulus-response or excitation-reaction relation will first of all be interpreted as adaptive necessity projected into a referential system—a system now commonly referred to as the "man-machine"—that represents the fusion of the scattered elements of the social mechanism, a fully-realized synthesis of the entire productive body. It was necessary for life to escape the body so that the concept of life, transformed through this metamorphosis, could rejoin the body in a dominated form and so that life's force, without losing any of its substance, could be absorbed by the power [*puissance*] of dead work. While this mechanistic conception of life bespeaks a continually renewed epistemological impulse, it also appears as a notable "symptom" of the productive body at its highest point of development. It is surely a single historical process that drives this twin destiny. In this case science does not reflect, but rather accompanies. Life's resistance necessitates the separation of the body within the man-machine construct, and it is this separation which allows and justifies, within this system, the discourse of the engineer of souls. Without this separation there would be no need whatsoever for scientific psychology, and, deprived of its function, the discipline would never have progressed beyond those imaginary experiments that marked the first steps of its infancy.[76]

3. Modern Psychology; or, New and Improved Productive Consumption

But in order for this separation to appear as the condition of an adequate discourse on the living machine, the machine had to be set free from human force and skill, a liberation that Marx saw as one of the conditions for the development of large-scale industry. In effect, this was the price that had to be paid for an "entirely objective and impersonal organism of production"[77] that could mark, despite the wished-for homogeneity, a radical separation between the dead machine and the living machine. The maintenance of the living machine therefore demands a specific discipline, to be built up from accredited research contributions that are initially physiological, but soon develop into psychology (notably those which concern the evaluation of sensory-motor and intellectual aptitudes). The productive complex requires the elaboration of a system that manages and perfects the various cogs in the mechanism: the worker becomes a mere "part" (as Marx puts it) of a machine which itself is only a working part, one element, of another machine, situated in the organizing movement of the general mechanism of production that is placed under the surveillance of engineers and mechanics (who will in turn be submitted to psychological controls and evaluation); and the entire system's intelligibility can only be located outside itself, on the level of capital. From now on the productive body will be constituted by the overall system of cogs that that make up the social mechanism. The biological body will be reduced, according the position of its subject in the division of labor, either to sensory organs that adapt themselves to the machine they serve, or to sensory or intellectual faculties that have the capacity—facilitated by ever-higher stages of technological evolution—to fulfill the functions of surveillance and control that are now required by the presence of the machine. The machine itself, the instrument of production, in the form of capital, is now transformed into dead work that dominates human force, depleting the biological body as it reduces it to the role of a slave dependent on a "lifeless mechanism." The intervention of Psychology will therefore be based on the inevitable need to manage this circuit. One way to understand it is in terms of what Marx called "productive consumption" as distinguished from "individual consumption," or the means of the workers subsistence, necessary to the reconstitution of his working force.[78] It is in between individual consumption (the basis of the individual's biological survival) and the maintenance (cleaning, repair, etc.) of dead machines that we find the space where this other understanding of the survival of the individual will be situated: modern psychology—in all its techniques of selection and detection, of aptitude development, of conditioning and learning, of preventing or absorbing conflict, of personality testing, etc.—can be considered as one of the key factors in the *improvement* of "productive consumption." The reality of the overall system's domination resides in this series of separated elements: the maintenance of dead machines corresponds to the maintenance of living machines on whom, on whose productive acts, the functioning of automatons as means of work depends.[79]

Whereas the life of the Cartesian body-machine was conquest, the life of the industrialized living machine is survival.

Consequently, the coexistence of these two aspects (the body reduced to a mechanical process; the inscription of the machine into a certain vital process) suddenly and clearly reveals the subjection of living beings to death. In the system of the fully-developed productive body, it is no longer the living being who runs the machine, but the machine that makes a machine out of the living being: "Capital," writes Marx, "absorbs living work 'as if it had the devil in its body'"[80]; it becomes monstrous.[81] This monstrosity is translated by deformity and mutilation of the body: the image of a body that is already "crippled," "mutilated," and broken [parcellarisé], in which "the individual himself is divided up, and transformed into the automatic motor of a detail operation," as in the fable of Agrippa,[82] is now supplanted—in the fulfillment of the system—by the image of a body reduced to the machine's "living isolated accessory,"[83] a body whose labor becomes a "a mere living accessory of this machinery."[84] Marked in its very body in this manner, the living machine is cast as a "linkage"[85]; its role is that of a cog that either serves or oversees the machine, that of an organ which is mechanical or intellectual (in the precise sense of tasks of surveillance and control), subjected to the criteria of labor time understood as the "quantity of work" and as the "sole determinant element" of production.[86] Far from being the living machine's means of labor, the dead machine imposes upon the living one the triple task of transmitting the machine's action to the raw material, surveilling that action, and guarding the machine against interruptions.[87] It is therefore the motion of dead machines that determines the activity of the living ones, and not the other way around. As capital, the "automatic mechanism... in the person of the capitalist" is animated by a single drive: "to reduce to a minimum the resistance offered by man, that obstinate yet elastic natural barrier."[88] As it emerges, the discipline of psychology comes to occupy a specific place, as part of this larger plan. The accessory, whether manual or intellectual, can never exceed the dimensions of the larger construction that actualizes its being. Its criteria of normality are therefore dependent on the intensive development—within prescribed limits—of this newly defined organ. Beyond that, the only option is surgery.

But the confiscation of life in the productive body is accompanied by a confiscation of knowledge [*savoir*] that signals a reinforcement of the division of labor: "The science which compels the inanimate limbs of the machinery, by their construction, to act purposefully, as an automaton, does not exist in the worker's consciousness, but rather acts upon him through the machine as an alien power, as the power of the machine itself."[89] This remark may be applied by analogy to the intervention of psychology: the living machine, reduced to the status of an accessory, constitutes a "moment"[90] of the productive process, but this "moment" is obviously dispossessed of the very meaning of its productive act because the accessory—which some dream of cutting back without harming the larger productive body, thereby misrecognizing the very structure of this body—in its essence, is not superfluity but ignorance. One of the functions of the psychological intervention (and more generally, of everything that gravitates around the idea of a "science of communication") is to restore to the subject an alien awareness of his condition by inculcating in him a certain type of self-awareness centered on folkloric notions of "belonging," of "feelings of group identity," or even a brand of "empathy-spontaneity-creativity" that lend a ludicrous aura to the concept of "personality," itself always accompanied by its trusty sidekick, "well-being" [*intégration*].[91]

Ure's description of the factory, taken up by Marx, as a "vast automaton, composed of various mechanical and intellectual organs, acting in uninterrupted concert for the production of a common object, all of them being subordinate to a self-regulating moving force"[92] provides a succinct image of the fully-developed productive body (Marx adds, "the automaton itself is the subject, and the workers are merely conscious organs,

coordinated with the unconscious organs of the automaton, and together with the latter subordinated to the central moving force") in its real functioning, even as it reproduces the ideal model of the productive body by lending credence to the illusion of a perfect co-operation of all the organs in the accomplishment of a single finality. This illusion may recall the way, in the Aristotelian universe, the hierarchical beings that make up the cosmos draw their persistence only from their imitation of divinity, the desirable *par excellence,* the first mover moving itself in eternal and circular motion, as pure form, pure act, the thought of thought, "separated" from itself in every sense of the term. It is for the maintenance of this illusion—which also expresses the effective tensions of the productive body, so that nothing may disturb the beautiful arrangement of the system thus established in its self-sufficiency—and in its interests, that psychology receives its call to duty.

We have attempted to show that the Galilean-Cartesian myth signals nothing else, on a certain level of analysis, than the emergence, in historical reality, of a possible discourse on production. This is one of the meanings of the theory of the body-machine which, as it confiscates the body's finality, develops the possibility of conceptualizing the productive body. At the other end of this chain, once the ruse that Cartesianism brings to light (without being its ultimate producer) is actualized, the discipline of psychology is nothing other, taken as a whole and in its multiple forms, than the discourse of production which is now economically necessary and historically possible: this is the reality of psychology. Or, if one prefers, through psychological discourses and practices (concerning aptitudes and learning, as well as mental pathology and personality), it is the productive body itself that speaks and acts, that discretely or spectacularly distills words and ideas—not without apparent contradictions—

which promote, recuperate, or sanitize, as they still do today on various levels and through a conspicuous politics, our active ideology, our vulgar economy, and our traditional or experimental pedagogy, etc. The productive body whispers, and these whispers radiate throughout all the sectors of everyday life; psychology is *one* of the real discourses of mastery over the productive body. The subject of psychology is therefore the productive body itself insofar as the biological body, the fundamental element of the productive body, requires a specific discourse through which, in a certain manner and with a certain tone, the entirety of the productive body expresses itself. At the same time, the intervention of the psychologist is marked by an immense ambiguity: in spite of and because of its premises, psychology is constituted as the most extreme effort to mechanize living beings, and as the necessary recognition of the failure of the total mechanization of life. The psychologist did not invent the living machine; but because this machine is *also* a living thing, the finality of the discipline is forced, in the end, to fall back on multiple conceptual and analogical supports imposed by the importation of a biological model into the heart of psychology itself. The "natural" problem of survival becomes a problem about the living being within the productive body, a two-fold problem in fact: there is individual consumption and there is productive consumption, and psychology takes charge of one aspect of the second category. The goals of psychology, which are no doubt distinct from those of the psychologist himself, are thereby integrated into the general goals of the productive body which, constrained as it is to tear life away from living beings in order to reduce them to desirable, machine-like acts, encounters at every step and in all its diverse forms the resistance of life—whether in class struggle, in the form of a resurgence of aspirations for living work, or, in everyday life, as demands for the recognition of alterity—and must, in consequence, and in the strongest sense, take account of it.

Notes

1. Tr. Note: François Jacob, *La logique du vivant; une histoire de l'hérédité* (Paris: Gallimard, 1970); English tr. *The Logic of Life: A History of Heredity* (Princeton: Princeton UP, 1993), tr. Betty E. Spillmann.

2. MacLuhan's periodization of our history into ages of communication—the oral age, the age of literacy, and finally the electronic age—in his *Understanding Media*, overvalorizes that power of mediation or communication that in reality corresponds only to a recent period, the modern period of a mercantile mode of production in which intermediaries seize a decisive role in the social order. This myth, retrospective by definition, justifies the valorization of a new age of technology in which production itself would vanish before the "message," as well as MacLuhan's general rejection of Marxism, which, within his conception of history, he accuses of failing to be grounded in phenomena of communication because grounded in those of production.

3. *Capital*, chapter 14, p. 459.

4. Ibid, p. 479.

5. Ibid.

6. *Capital*, chapter 13, p. 443.

7. *Capital*, chapter 13, pp. 448-49 [translation slightly modified].

8. Ibid. [translation slightly modified].

9. *Capital*, chapter 13, pp. 449-50 [translation modified].

10. Particularly in all the versions of Trotskyism that rely on the fully-developed productive body, on machinification, to denounce capital's parasitism on production, and reverse or replace it. This is the economistic version of Marxism, with a vengeance.

11. *Capital*, chapter 13, pp. 449-50.

12. This point is developed in Part Two of this study.

13. This problem will be developed in Part Two.
14. *Capital*, chapter 14, pp. 489-90.
15. Ibid, chapter 14, p. 481; see all of section 5, "The Capitalist Character of Manufacture." [Tr. note: Marx draws this example closely from Smith, *Wealth of Nations*: B.I, Ch.11, "Of the Rent of Land"].
16. Ibid, chapter 15, p. 494.
17. Ibid, chapter 15, p. 497: "...it is purely accidental that the motive power [*force*] happens to be clothed in the form of human muscles."
18. Ibid, chapter 15, pp. 495-96.
19. Ibid, chapter 15, p. 499.
20. Ibid, p. 503.
21. Ibid, p. 508.
22. Ibid, p. 508.
23. In *Connaissance de la vie* [Knowledge of Life; 1952], in the essay "Aspects of Vitalism," Georges Canguilhem compares mechanism to the Hegelian ruse of reason.
24. Edmund Husserl, *The Crisis of European Sciences and Transcendental Phenomenology: an Introduction to Phenomenological Philosophy*. Translated by David Carr. Evanston: Northwestern University Press, 1970 (originally written 1934-37 and published 1954), p. 49-50.
25. Ibid, 51.
26. Ibid, 51.
27. Ibid, 54.
28. Ibid, 60.
29. Ibid, 63.
30. Maurice Merleau-Ponty, *Phenomenology of Perception*. Translated by Colin Smith. New York: Routledge, 2002 (originally published 1945), p. 106.
31. Ibid, 109.
32. This is the well-known theme of the rejection of the natural finality and spontaneity that were exalted by Renaissance

thought, the banishment of the marvelous, and the promotion of equilibrium. In the same gesture, simple subsistence is replaced by limitless production, production for production's sake (the rehabilitation of usury, the condemnation of laziness replaces that of avarice), etc.

33. We take this term from R. Lenoble, *Histoire de l'idée de nature*, collection "Evolution de l'humanité," (Paris: Albin Michel, 1969), p. 326.

34. The construction of the image of the body, not as an instrument of knowledge [*savoir*] but as the recognition of a mechanical power [*pouvoir*], implies that bodily experience is initially apprehended only in its apparently aberrant forms: false sensations, phantom limbs, dreams, or madness.

35. Cf. the letter to Mesland of 9 February, 1645. Pléiade edition, p. 1174.

36. Cf. Georges Canguilhem, *La Connaissance de la vie* [Knowledge of Life] (Paris: Vrin, 1967), p. 113.

37. See Georges Canguilhem, *Descartes et la technique* [Descartes and Technics], IXeme Congrès internationale de Philosophie, II. Etudes cartésiennes, IIe partie (Paris; Hermann, 1937), p. 84: "And 'since we cannot make ourselves a new body,' we must add exterior organs to our interior organs (VII, 148); and artificial organs to natural organs (VII, 165). It is in the needs, appetites, and will that we must seek the initial impulse toward technological manufacturing (IX, *Principes*, 123)."

38. Cf. Georges Canguilhem, *La connaissance de la vie*, p. 115: "According to Descartes, an executive mechanical apparatus replaces the power [*pouvoir*] of direction and command, but God has determined direction once and for all; the constructor has included direction of movement in the executive mechanical apparatus."

39. Cf. Marx, Letter to Engels of 28 January, 1863:"*The industrial revolution* begins as soon as mechanical means were employed

in fields where, from time immemorial, the final result had called for human labor, and not, therefore... where the actual material to be processed had *never, within living memory*, been directly connected with the human hand; where, by the nature of things and from the outset, man has not functioned purely as **power** ["power" in English in the original German; Marx and Engels, *Collected Works*, (New York: International Publishers, 1975), v. 41, p. 451].

40. Tr. note: Three-wheeled "tortoises" designed to seek light by William Grey Walter (1910-77); these devices, built in 1948-49, were among the first electronic autonomous robots.

41. This is cybernetics as "the art of making action efficacious," a definition that Henri Laborit reaffirms with respect to biology. See "La cybernétique et la machine humaine" ["Cybernetics and the Human Machine"], in *Le dossier de la cybernétique* (Paris: Marabout, 1967), p. 195.

42. *The Condition of the Working Class in England*, CW vol. 4, p. 312.

43. This occurs very early in the process, for example in Laffemas' attempt to fill his workshop with "little children, the blind, old amputees and the helpless, all sitting around comfortably, without working or exerting themselves" (cf. H Hauser, *Les débuts du Capitalisme* [The Beginnings of Capitalism], Paris: Alcan, 1927, p. 12.). This particular investment in the suffering, pain-ridden, mutilated body or feeble constitution, seen as an indication of special aptitude for the mechanical gesture that reduces physical effort, is a notable aspect of the system. In the generalization of competition, capitalism marks the body in this way (and many others) as it recuperates hitherto unsuspected potentials. As the productive body is enlarged, so too is the field of exploitation of the biological body. For more on this subject, see Marx, *Capital* I, chapter 15, section 3a, pp. 517ff. ["Appropriation of Supplementary Labor Power by Capital:

The Employment of Women and Children" and following sections]. The extension of the productive body goes hand in hand with the limitation of the productive act: "The one-sidedness and even the deficiencies of the specialized individual worker become perfections when he is part of the collective worker. The habit of doing only one thing converts him into an organ which operates with the certainty of a force of nature, while his connection with the whole mechanism compels him to work with the regularity of a piece of machinery" (*Capital*, chapter 14, p. 469).

44. Cf. Marx, *Grundrisse*, p. 704: it is "the division of labor, which gradually transforms the workers' operations into more and more mechanical ones, so that at a certain point a machine can step into their places."

45. Cf. Descartes, Letter to Régius, January 1642 in *Lettres à Régius* (Paris: Vrin, 1959), p. 8 9; and *Principes* IV, p. 203. See also Géraud de Cordemoy [1626-84], *Oeuvres Philosophiques* ([Pierre Clair and François Girbal, eds.,] Paris: Presses Universitaires de France, 1968), p. 122, 3rd Discours, "Des machines naturelles et artificielles" ["Of Natural and Artificial Machines"]: "Everything that we admire in works of Art or of Nature is a pure effect of that motion and arrangement, which, in accordance with their diversity, makes them suitable for their different usages."

46. Cf. Descartes, *Traité des passions* [*de l'âme*], articles 5-6. See also Georges Canguilhem, *La formation du concept de réflexe aux XVIIe et XVIIIe siècles* [The Formation of the Concept of Reflection in the 17th and 18th Centuries] (Paris: Presses Universitaires de France, 1955), p. 55.

47. Cf. Georges Canguilhem, *La connaissance de la vie*, pp. 106 ff., and Alexandre Koyré, *Etudes d'histoire de la pensée scientifique* (Paris: Presses Universitaires de France, 1966), p. 148, note 3.

48. The persistent ambiguity is inevitable: animal action, the quintessence of the mechanical act, is seen as the height of

promptness, precision, and efficacy, precisely insofar as it is not the consequence of deliberation. In this case slowness and uncertainty are the characteristics of reason. This is the argument developed by Pierre Chanet in *Considérations sur la sagesse de Charon* [Considerations on the Wisdom of Charon] (1643). See J.B. Piobetta, *Au temps de Descartes, une polémique ignorée sur la connaissance des animaux* [In Descartes' time: A forgotten polemic on the knowledge of animals], IXe Congrès International de la Philosophie, II, Etudes cartésiennes, IIe partie (Paris: Editions Hermann, 1937), p. 62.

49. In *De pulsu, resorptione, auditu, et tactu: annotationes anatomicae et physiologicae* [Of the pulse, resorption, hearing, and touch: anatomical and physiological notes] (Leipzig, 1834), "Prolegomena XI," E. H. Weber explains that the sense of touch reveals: 1) The force of resistance that our bodies oppose to the pressure of our organs; 2) the shape of bodies and the space that separates them; 3) the force with which our body compresses our organs, particularly its weight; 4) the body's temperature, whether hot or cold.

50. E. Toulouse and H. Piéron, *Technique de Psychologie expérimentale*, 2nd ed. (Paris: Editions Doin, 1911), vol. I, p. 34.

51. See J.J. Van Biervliet, *La psychologie quantitative* (2e étude, "La psychophysiologie," *Revue philosophique*, June 1907, pp. 565-66.

52. For a precise definition of parallelism, see Théodule Ribot, *Introduction à la Psychologie allemande contemporaine* (Paris: Alcan, 1879) pp, IX and XI ; and Wilhelm Wundt, *Elements de psychologie physiologique*, E. Rouvier, trans. (Paris: Alcan, 1886), vol. II, p. 521.

53. See A. Godfernaux, "Le parallélisme psycho-physique et ses conséquences," *Revue philosophique* 2 (1904), pp. 329-52 and 482-504.

54. See Wundt, *Eléments de psychologie physiologique*, vol. I, p. 9. See also the definition of "soul" ["*âme*"] in vol. II, p. 526: "the absolute correlation of the psychic and the physical suggests

the following hypothesis: what we call the soul is the internal being [*être*] of the same unity, a unity that we envision externally as being [*étant*] the body, which belongs to it."

55. Gustav T. Fechner, *Elemente der Psychophysik* (Leipzig, 1860) [Elements of Psychophysics, trans. Helmut Adler (New York: Holt, Rinehart and Winston, 1966), p. 7]. See also chapter VII, "The Principle of Psychophysical Measurement," on Fechner's hope for devising laws of the senses that would be as important for understanding soul-body relations as the law of gravity for understanding celestial motion.

56. Compare Van Biervliet, *La Psychologie quantitative*, p. 579.

57. J. J. Van Biervliet, *La Psychologie quantitative*, p. 591.

58. Godfernaux, "Le parallélisme psycho-physique et ses conséquences, "p. 343. See also Jean Piaget, "L'explication en psychologie et le parallélisme psychophysiologique," in Fraisse and Piaget, *Traité de Psychologie expérimentale*, 1ere Partie, "Histoire et Méthode"(Paris: Presse Universitaire de France, 1967, p. 152). Here Piaget shows how Edouard Clarapède formulated a law "according to which consciousness awakens as a result of disadaptations." For Clarapède's discussion of this law, see his article "La Psychologie fonctionelle," in *Revue philosophique*, January 1933, p. 14. See also pp. 5-6, where he writes: "Psychology is a part of biology.... The central problem of biology is that of *adaptation*.... And the central problem of psychology is that of *behavior*. But behavior is nothing but a certain species of adaptation."

In a text that develops the consequences of a polemic against Auguste Comte and that intends to preserve the status of "subjectivity," Herbert Spencer writes: "The claims of psychology to rank as a distinct science, are thus not smaller but greater than those of any other science. If its phenomena are considered objectively, merely as neuro-muscular adjustments, by which the higher organisms from moment to moment adapt their actions to environing coexistants and sequences, its degree of specificity even then, entitles it to a separate place. The moment the element of feeling, or consciousness, is used to interpret these neuro-muscular adjustments in the living beings around it, objective Psychology acquires an additional and quite exceptional distinction. And it is further distinguished in being linked by this common element of consciousness, to the totally independent science of subjective Psychology—the two forming a double science, which, as a whole, is quite *sui generis;*" *The Principles of Psychology* (New York: D. Appleton, 1872), p. 141.

59. Godfernaux, "Le parallélisme psycho-physique et ses conséquences," p. 499.

60. See H. Hoffding, *Esquisse d'une psychologie fondée sur l'expérience* (1882), trans. L. Poitevin (Paris : Alcan, 1900), p. 18. [Tr. note: This programmatic phrase also appears in William James, *Principles of Psychology* (1890), ch. 1, parag. 1].

61. Jean-François Richard, "La découverte du fait des différances individuelles comme obstacle dans les premières expériences de mesure en psychologie," part of a colloquium on "l'Elaboration des concepts et des méthodes de la psychologie différentielle au XIXe siècle et au debut du XXe siècle." In *Revue de Synthèse : Colloques, textes des rapports* (Paris: Albin Michel, 1968), pp. 369-82; see also pp. 375, 381.

62. Pierre Bouguer, *Traité d'optique sur la gradation de la lumière* (Paris: Guerin et Delatour, 1760), Livre I, section 2, article 1, p. 51. This development points toward the category of average social labor, whose level is never a permanent attainment and thus demands the worker's constant striving. See for example, Marx, "Results of the Immediate Process of Production" [Tr. note: published as an "Appendix" in the Penguin edition of *Capital*]: "...the worker must perform the *normal social* quantity of useful labor in a

given time. The capitalist therefore compels him to work at the normal social *average* rate of intensity" (*Capital*, 987).

63. Toulouse and Piéron, *Technique de psychologie expérimentale*, vol. I, p. 214.
64. Ibid., p. 242.
65. Dewey writes: "The ability of the hand to do its work will depend, either directly or indirectly, upon its control, as well as its stimulation, by the act of vision"; see "The Reflex Arc Concept in Psychology," *The Psychological Review* 3:4 (July, 1896), p. 359.
66. Denis Diderot, "Eléments de physiologie," in *Œuvres complètes de Diderot* (Paris: Garnier Belles-Lettres, 1875), vol. IX, pp. 344-45.
67. Tr. note: accommodation, in this usage, is "the action or power of adapting the eyes to view objects at various distances" (OED).
68. See Dewey, "The Reflex Arc Concept in Psychology," p. 370.
69. See James R. Angell, "The province of functional psychology," *Psychological Review* 14 (1907), pp. 61-91: "The functional psychologist then in his modern attire is interested not alone in the operations of mental process considered merely of and by and for itself, but also and more vigorously in mental activity as part of a larger stream of biological forces which are daily and hourly at work before our eyes...." (p. 68). Similarly, William James: "...*mental life is primarily teleological*, that is to say that our various ways of feeling and thinking have grown to be what they are because of their utility in shaping our *reactions* to the outer world. On the whole, few recent formulas have done more service in psychology than the Spencerian one that the essence of mental life and of bodily life are one, namely, 'the adjustment of inner to outer relations.'... Primarily then, and fundamentally, the mental life is for the sake of action of a preservative sort" [*Psychology: Briefer Course* [1892] (Cambridge: Harvard

UP, 1984, pp. 11-12)]. This problem of finality or teleology also preoccupies Edouard Clarapède in the aforementioned article: "the fact of considering organic and mental processes in relation to their end and their utility strikes many as teleological thinking"; but (1) "functional psychology in no wise contradicts mechanistic explanations" (p. 7) and (2) "the functional point of view implies no adherence to teleologism. If we can explain these adaptive coordinations in an entirely mechanical fashion, so much the better! (For the mechanistic explanation is always more pleasing to the mind)" (p. 17).

70. James M. Cattell, "Mental Tests and Measurements," *Mind* 15 (1890), 373.

71. Tr. Note: Cattell's original English phrase "bodily power" is given in French as "vigeur corporelle." Consequently this phrase is not involved in lexicon of *pouvoir, puissance, force, energie.*

72. See Part One of this study for development of this point.

73. The most important phenomenon in Taylorism seems to be "the substitution of a science for the individual judgment of the workman" (114). See Frederick W. Taylor, *Principles of Scientific Management* (1911) [in *Scientific management: comprising Shop management, The principles of scientific management and Testimony before the special House committee, with a forward by Harlow S. Person* (New York: Harper, 1947)]. Besides Taylor's obvious concerns—the struggle against loafing, the need to select personnel on the basis of ability and amenability, the collaboration between classes now referred to as "the intimate cooperation of the management with the workman, so that they together do the work in accordance with the scientific laws which have been developed, instead of leaving the solution of each problem in the hands of the individual workman" (115), and thus "the accurate study of the motives which influence men"

(119) and the need for "a complete change in the mental attitude of all the men in the shop toward their work and toward their employers" (100-01; see also 30-31, 93, 131-32) so as to substitute peace for war on the shop floor; besides the outright cynicism laced with naiveté that screams from every page of his testimony before the House special committee in 1912, whether in Taylor's leadership of a team charged with determining the norm for a "proper day's work" (123, 143-44, 179, 222) or in his advocacy of manipulative practices tied to raises and promotions ("incentive" [36-39]); and in fact besides the outrageous statements he blithely proffers on the worker-machine relation (a typical example: "In working on the average machine tool, of necessity the greater part of the day is spent by the man standing at his machine doing nothing except watch his machine work. I think I would be safe in saying that not more than three hours of actual physical work would be the average that any machinist would have to do in running his machine—not more than three hours' actual physical work in the day. The rest of the time the machine is working and he simply stands there watching it. So there is no fear of overwork in the machine shop" [124-25].), a more instructive aspect of his thinking seems to be the way it opens up the possibility of treating the manual laborer as a trainable "gorilla" [40] and consequently of assuming that proper adaptation to a defined task will necessarily remain completely unintelligible to the worker who accomplishes it, since the overall process has been broken down into its elementary mechanisms, this latter task being reserved for a managerial specialist, the competent man, the engineer of souls. It is hardly surprising, therefore, that the model for this emerging "science" should be the engineer of the body, the modern surgeon, who spontaneously applies the principles of scientific management in his professional

practice. He is "the man who combines the greatest manual dexterity and skill with the largest amount of intellectual attainment" (197). Is there any need to write an epilogue here on the fact that the surgeon is the one who achieves therapeutic ends by amputating and replacing parts? In any event, it is notable that science is perfectly integrated into the development of the productive body at this point; not as a simple ideology of productivity, but rather as a constitutive element of the productive body itself. In this sense, Taylorism only *reinforces* the position of modern psychology. And indeed, this integration had been an explicit goal for some time already, for example in Andrew Ure's early nineteenth-century writings: "By the infirmity of human nature it happens that the more skillful the workman, the more self-willed and intractable he is apt to become, and, of course, the less fit a component of a mechanical system, in which by occasional irregularities he may do great damage to the whole. The grand object of the modern manufacturer is, through the union of capital and science, to reduce the task of his work-people to the exercise of vigilance and dexterity" (quoted in J.A.C. Brown, *The Social Psychology of Industry: Human Relations in the Factory* [New York: Penguin, 1954], 208). [Added by Didier Deleule, 2006: Marx quotes this passage in *The Poverty of Philosophy*, p. 189 (CW, vol. 9).].

74. Quoted in Marx, *Capital* I, chapter 25, p. 806.

75. Contemporary psychology does not deny conflict and in fact gives it a fundamental role. But it displaces the notion of conflict into psychological spheres (whether personal or interpersonal) and tends to universalize this mode of displacement. This might be an obvious observation today, but whether we call it regression or displacement, it still merits our attention here, if only to recall a time, not so long ago, when such a gesture was still questionable.

76. The diverse projects of Wolff, Ramsay, Crusius, Maupertius,

Ploucquet, Bonnet, Mérian, Hagen, Kürber, all gathered under the rubric of "psychometry," remain at the level of programmatic plans; none of them actually enters the realm of experimentation (see K. Ramul, "The Problem of Measurement in the Psychology of the Eighteenth Century," *American Psychologist* 15 (1960), pp. 256-265). What actually triumphs in the psychology of the eighteenth century is imaginary experimentation, and it does so on two levels: (1) The question posed by Molyneux in his March 2, 1692 letter to Locke (*Works of John Locke*, 7th ed., London, 1768, vol. 4, p. 282), a question that Locke will insert in the second, 1693 edition of the *Essay* (II.IX.8), provides a good example of the first level at which it is understood. This "jocose problem," to use Molyneux's phrase, formulates a question that will elicit an immediate response that can easily avoid passing through the detour of real experience (and the fact that the experiment was actually carried out by Cheselden in 1728—in conditions that did not allow certainty in the response— changes nothing). From the start, Molyneux's problem becomes a metaphysical experience for metaphysicians, a kind of parlor game that is almost a "riddle" (Molyneux notes at the beginning of his letter that he has posed his question to several people in the course of his ordinary encounters). While Molyneux takes no explicit stand against real experimentation in his letter, neither does he ever envisage it; the lapidary response he brings to the question he himself has posed is, in fact, an index of the way he dispenses with experimentation. Molyneux's *query* is incontestably a question of pure reasoning as far as he is concerned, and this is certainly the way Locke understands it. (2) The "metaphysical" experiment, in the sense that Maupertuis understands it (see "Lettre sur le progrès des sciences," paragraph XVII, in *Oeuvres de Maupertuis*, Lyon, 1768, vol. 2, pp. 426-30), may constitute the second level at which the authors cited above are attached to this notion. In examples such as the artificial production of dreams through drugs, or the artificial isolation of a few children in order to shed light on the production of language, experimentation may be considered as something desirable. The philosopher's goal here is never to take any kind of actual experimental risks, however, but rather to achieve a sort of technical success in the context of his polemic. To explain this "lack" of experimentation by invoking a *Zeitgeist*, as does P. Fraisse via Boring (in Fraisse and Piaget, *Traité de psychologie expérimentale, Histoire et Méthode*, 2nd ed.; Paris, P.U.F.: 1967; p. 11) is simply to avoid the problem.

77. Marx, *Capital* I, chapter 15, p. 508 [translation modified].
78. Ibid, I, chapter 23, p. 717: "The worker's consumption is of two kinds. While producing he consumes the means of production with his labor, and converts them into products with a higher value than that of the capital advanced. This is his productive consumption. It is at the same time consumption of his labour-power by the capitalist who has bought it. On the other hand, the worker uses the money paid to him for his labor-power to buy the means of subsistence; this is his individual consumption."
79. See the distinction from Potter, discussed by Marx (in chapter 23, pp. 720 ff.), between "inanimate machinery" that wears out and loses value from day to day "owing to constant technical progress" (722), and "living machinery" that, on the contrary, "gets better the longer it lasts, and in proportion as the skill handed down from one generation to another accumulates" (722); this "skill," as Marx notes earlier, is viewed by the capitalist "as the real existence of his variable capital" (720).
80. Marx, *Grundrisse*, p. 704 [Tr. note: Marx is citing a line from Goethe, *Faust* Part I, Act III. The French (Rubel) translation of *Capital* gives a different line from Goethe than the English

(Fowkes) tr. in Penguin, p. 74, which cites Part I, Act V to very different effect, i.e., " as though its body were by love possessed."].

81. Marx returns often to this image of monstrosity. See for example *Grundrisse*, p. 470 ("Machinery, or fixed capital, which, as animated monster, fixes the scientific idea"); *Capital* chapter 14, p. 481 (where the worker is converted into "a crippled monstrosity"); *Capital* chapter 15, p. 503 ("Here we have, in place of the isolated machine, a mechanical monster whose gigantic body fills whole factories...."); or chapter 15, p. 618 ("That monstrosity, the disposable working population, held in reserve, in misery, for the changing requirements of capitalist exploitation.").

82. "Man as a mere fragment of his own body"; see *Capital,* chapter 14, pp. 481-82.

83. *Grundrisse*, p. 470.

84. Ibid, p. 693.

85. Ibid, p. 692.

86. Ibid, p. 700.

87. Ibid, p. 692.

88. *Capital,* chapter 15, p. 527.

89. *Grundrisse*, p. 693. On the forced acceleration of scientific development as a productive form, see not only this section of the *Grundrisse* (692-706), but also *Capital,* 482, 508, 799.

90. See *Grundrisse*, p. 699: "Hence the tendency of capital to give production a scientific character; direct labor [is] reduced to a mere moment of this process."

91. For more, see our article, "Le philosophe et le psychologue," in *Revue philosophique*, January-March 1971, pp. 19 ff., as well as the second part of *La psychologie, mythe scientifique* (Paris: Ed. Robert Laffont, coll. "Libertés," 1969).

92. *Capital,* chapter 15, p. 544.

Contemporary culture has eliminated both the concept of the public and the figure of the intellectual. Former public spaces – both physical and cultural – are now either derelict or colonized by advertising. A cretinous anti-intellectualism presides, cheerled by expensively educated hacks in the pay of multinational corporations who reassure their bored readers that there is no need to rouse themselves from their interpassive stupor. The informal censorship internalized and propagated by the cultural workers of late capitalism generates a banal conformity that the propaganda chiefs of Stalinism could only ever have dreamt of imposing. Zer0 Books knows that another kind of discourse – intellectual without being academic, popular without being populist – is not only possible: it is already flourishing, in the regions beyond the striplit malls of so-called mass media and the neurotically bureaucratic halls of the academy. Zer0 is committed to the idea of publishing as a making public of the intellectual. It is convinced that in the unthinking, blandly consensual culture in which we live, critical and engaged theoretical reflection is more important than ever before.